THE FREEDOM GAME

The Freedom Game - Copyright © 2018 by R. A. Blumenthal

Soft cover ISBN: 978-1-62432-030-9
eBook ISBN: 978-1-62432-031-6

BISAC Subject Headings:
SOC054000   SOCIAL SCIENCE / Slavery
YAF001000   YOUNG ADULT FICTION / Action & Adventure / General
YAF052030   YOUNG ADULT FICTION / Romance / Historical

Please address all correspondence to:

Loose Leaves Publishing, LLC
4218 E. Allison Road
Tucson, AZ 85712

Or visit our website at:
www.LooseLeavesPublishing.com

THE FREEDOM GAME

BY

R. A. BLUMENTHAL

A NOTE FROM THE AUTHOR

Before the American Civil War, Native Americans of the Indian Territory, including people of the Cherokee Nation, owned thousands of slaves. The Cherokee Council codified slavery and enacted slave laws which included severe punishments, but the desire for freedom could not be extinguished. *The Freedom Game* was inspired by the actual events of the Slave Revolt of 1842, when twenty-five slaves made a daring escape from a Cherokee plantation. The book imagines the details of such an event, as well as the personalities of those who might have participated.

Today, the descendants of those slaves struggle to achieve formal recognition as part of the Native American nations among whom their ancestors lived and worked.

There are many authentic slave memoirs and narratives written in a voice as articulate as the main character of *The Freedom Game*, though most people of the place and period described may not have been able to express themselves as readily. To faithfully convey some of the characters' thoughts and feelings to the modern reader, it seemed necessary to use a more standard form of speech than a strictly historical dialect, as one might translate any material from the original language into that of the reader.

Finally, in writing this book, I hoped to honor the twenty-five souls who risked their lives in the pursuit of freedom.

RICHARD A. BLUMENTHAL

CHAPTER 1

Slowly, my son spun himself around, his small, brown arm outstretched, his hand pointing to the unkempt graves all around us. "Pa, why do all of those people have big, flat rocks with names on them?" He stopped his arm at the bare graves in front of where we stood, "And these don't?" He looked up at me, his hand still pointing. "Why not, Pa?"

He was right. They didn't. The old cemetery with its uneven rows and overgrown grave beds was hardly distinguishable from the light brown fields that surrounded us. It could be identified as a burial ground only by the headstones that named each and every person buried there, except for these five mounds. "That's exactly why we're here, son. You're very smart to notice it." I crouched down to look at him face-to-face. "I love the people buried in these graves that have no names, and I want them to have stones that say who they are, like the other graves have."

"Why don't they have their names?" he asked.

I wanted him to know their story, so I was happy that he asked. "When they died, a long time ago, before you and your sister were born, the people who buried them didn't want them to be remembered. They wanted my friends to be completely forgotten. That's why they have no stones with their names. But you know what? I remember them anyway. I remember them very well."

"Why didn't you give your friends some stones then? Were the stones too heavy?"

Why not then was another good question. It went right to the heart of the matter. Simple answers don't work for my son. "It wasn't because the stones were too heavy. Your mother and I were far away from Webb's Bend when my friends were buried here. We were hiding from the people who

1

buried them." As the words came out of my mouth, I realized what a poor explanation that was for him. There was so much more to it and he deserved to know. I had to find the right way to tell him about this.

"Hiding, Pa? Like when we hid from the storm?"

Where we live, sometimes the sky turns almost black, with green clouds. When it does, you have to run for a safe place and pray that the finger of the storm passes by without touching you and yours, because, if it does, it can kill. It's as if a horrible finger from the sky is pointing to whatever spot on the Earth has been marked for destruction. Jumping Ben, one of the five people buried here, used to call such a storm an unole.

"It was a different kind of danger," I told him. "They were searching for us because they wanted to hurt us. So, Momma and I hid from them." His expression turned to one of concern. He must have thought they were still after us. "Not anymore, though. Nothing for you to worry about, now."

"Good, Pa. It's too nice a day to hide." He laughed and ran through the rows as though the cemetery was his personal playground.

Today, I feel a natural calm in the air. I feel safe, settled. I am not running from anyone or anything, as I have done for so much of my adult life. Instead, I am sheltered by the serenely sweet blue sky of a mid-November morning in the Indian Territory, like being beneath a protective dome. Yet, even under this peaceful dome, there can be stark weather variations. Take a few steps one way and you stand out in the bright sunshine; the skin on your hands and face can get warm, almost hot. Then, if you take a few steps inside the shade of a tree, you'll be chilled. If there's a wind, you'll be cold. It's one extreme or the other. Not all that long ago, that's what life was like in Webb's Bend for more than just the weather. People were choosing sides for every-thing, arguing about everything, sometimes with a deadly result. Life has calmed down considerably since then, and, just now, I feel the slow-drifting, pungent, damp air that hovers low over the Arkansas River, carried through Webb's Bend.

I had visited this cemetery and two other old graveyards like it some weeks ago, examining the graves carefully. I was hoping to find five togeth-er, unmarked by the naming stones that graves normally wear. When I saw these five, all in a row, I was sure I had the right ones. Rich folk and poor folk of all sorts are buried in this ground. The names of both free and slave tell the contents of the graves, and I see plenty of names I grew up with. Some were buried at around the same time that these unmarked graves were dug, another clue that I'm in the right place. Other, familiar names of those who died in the War Between the States are buried in their own section. Strange, how this place seems to level everything out between slave and free. In life, these people were ruled by unbending, ruthless laws and customs, designed to separate the free from the slave in every way. Before the war, the laws of the Cherokee Nation set out what slaves were forbidden to do, along with what the punishment would be if a slave broke that law, right down to the number of lashes that were to be administered by the Light-horse police for each offense. One law stated that slaves must never be taught how to read or write. Another one made it a crime for slaves to own anything, not a horse, not a cabin, not even a pair of shoes. Everything slaves used, ate, or wore was the property of their owner, just as a slave was the property of the owner.

I had traveled to Tahlequah and paid in advance for stone markers to be engraved with the names I want remembered. The man had been surprised when, in front of him, I easily wrote the names that were to be carved into the rock. Seeing me, obviously a former slave, write so fluently, he couldn't have been more amazed if I had performed a magic trick. I'm used to that. He took my money and scheduled the stones to be delivered.

We heard wagon wheels rolling into the cemetery grounds. The wagon was pulled by a single ox and carried two men with the headstones. I took off my hat and waved it high in the air to catch their attention.

"Over here," I called. "Over here."

The wagon pulled up noisily, as close as the driver could get it to the end of the row, and the two men jumped off. The ox found something on the ground to chew. The men walked over to have a look at where they would be working. "Sorry about those squeaky wheels, mister. Truth is, I'm gettin' a bit squeaky myself, lately," the older of the two said jokingly.

"I reckon you could use a little more axle grease. On the wheels, that is," I said with a laugh. Then I got right to business. "These five are the graves for the stones in your wagon. There's no particular order for them. I don't truly know who goes where. However you set them will have to do."

The older man was staring at my face, as though he were searching far back into his memory. "Hey," he said. "Do I know you?" He paused, thoughtfully. "I think I do. Hold on a minute. And these names, on these stones? I thought they looked kind of familiar." He stood quietly looking at me for a moment, piecing it all together in his mind. In a reverent whisper he said, "Yup. 18 hundred and 42. Am I right?" He pointed a finger at me. "You're the one that could read, ain't you? Am I right? Well, I swear." He was grinning. "You're him. Well, I swear."

His partner asked, "What happened in 1842, Bill? Who is this?"

"It's a long story, Linus. I'll tell you on the way back." He couldn't stop smiling and shaking his head, hardly believing what he was seeing. "Imagine that. After all these years. I was there, too. God bless you, boy. God bless." He looked at my son. "Your Daddy is a great man. A great man. God bless." I thanked him for his kindness, grateful that he understood the importance of the work he was doing. They began unloading the wagon, the man looking over his shoulder at me from time to time.

His memory was good. He recognized me and he knew that I was the one who could read. That meant a lot to me, personally, and it also showed me that I wasn't the only one still living who remembered what happened in 1842. I'm sure there are even more freed slaves somewhere, who were with us then, though most are probably getting pretty old. They could tell their versions of what happened, as this man will tell his partner later, but they can only speak their recollections, passing the story on by word of mouth. When they are gone, perhaps buried in that very cemetery, their voices will also be gone and the story might be gone along with them. I can't let that happen. I can do more, because I'm the only slave who was there who can write it down, preserving it. That one, special time my being able to read changed our lives forever is the reason why now it's up to me to tell the story. If I can do something that no one else can do, something this important, I just feel like I have to do it.

People are always wondering, sometimes out loud, sometimes with a look of disbelief like the man in Tahlequah who I hired to carve the head-stones, if the law prohibited all slaves from learning to read and write, how did I come to be the only slave in Webb's Bend who could? It was the woman who owned me, Missus Vanner. She taught me. Missus was the Cherokee mistress of the Vanner plantation, one of the biggest and richest in the Cherokee part of the Indian Territory. She seemed to take a liking to me from the first. I was very young when she started paying special attention to me.

She wanted me around her, all the time. Missus would bring me with her on her errands to various parts of the plantation, to stores in town, everywhere she went, I'd be with her. When I was little, she would have me play next to her on the floor as she worked at her desk in what I used to call her business room, in the big house. What's more, when I was openly curious, she would explain to me what she was doing and how she was doing it. One day, in response to one of my many queries, she said, "Boy, you ask a lot of good questions. You're a smart one, I think. I can use a smart one to help me out." She held her chin in her hand for a moment, looking at me. "I'm going to teach you how to read and how to write and how to cipher numbers. That way, you can help me run this place. Would you like that?" I grinned. I didn't know what to say. "Okay then, Book Boy, let's get started." She sat me at a table and with a patience I didn't think she had, Missus taught me the alphabet right then and there. I was thrilled! And I liked my new name, too. Book Boy. Soon, everyone would know me as Book Boy. As I grew and learned, I was able to accomplish just about anything that Missus needed me to do. She would send me on most errands alone, even to town, confident that I would complete the task well and return to her on the plantation when it was finished.

For a while, I thought that she might even be my mother. I don't think so now, but as a young boy, I almost believed it. The problem with that theory was that I didn't think Mr. Money Joe Vanner, Missus's husband, the master of the plantation, was my father. He hardly ever looked at me. Though, unlike most of his slaves, he allowed my presence in almost any room of the big house, as though I were a kind of pet. He tolerated me as he would Missus's pet dog. I was living firmly in the domain of Missus and that was okay by me because Mr. Money Joe scared me. He regularly bellowed orders to the other slaves and expected immediate obedience or harsh discipline would follow. Compared to other plantations I've since heard of, he treated us better than most, but that doesn't mean I didn't witness some very bloody lashings. Mr. Money Joe always had one of the overseers administer the punishment. They would boast that the scars they left would be a reminder to all the slaves that they had better do what they were told, as though they were doing us some kind of favor with the whip. We hated them.

Of course, many things have changed since then. I grew up on the Vanner place a slave and now I've returned to Webb's Bend a free man. On the losing side of the War Between the States, the Cherokee Nation was forced to free slaves like me. Now, I can come and go as I please, more or less, yet I've returned by my own choice. I'm not sure why. Maybe the natural beauty that still graces Webb's Bend has drawn me back to this corner of the Indian Territory after all these years. It's a small town, named for its founder, John Webb, who was one of the first of the Cherokees to leave his home in the east and move to the Indian Territory. He chose this spot because it lay near a bend in the Arkansas River, where there would be abundant fishing and easy transportation by boat. The woods were full of game animals, nut trees, berries and honey. He saw that the land was green and fertile here, that it would easily support farms, large and small, some as large as the plantations he must have known back east. As Webb's Bend grew into a community, it thrived on the wealth and commerce that the local plantations brought; wealth created in part from the sweat and blood of the hundreds of slaves who worked for their Cherokee masters. Yet, most Cherokee people either owned no slaves at all, or maybe one or two. There were the small farming families whose crops were tended with their own hands. There were the woods people who lived in dirt floor cabins, often set on cleared land near the river, cabins built by the people who lived in them. They were constructed of the rough lumber sawn from the cleared trees. They lived just as pioneers had lived all across the western frontier. Still others were skilled in the various trades and professions that keep a village running, even a small one. Webb's Bend had just one main street to speak of, with uncomplicated buildings spread out along a single dirt road that was dusty in dry weather and muddy in wet. Reverend Watson's Baptist church and Grady's General Store are the buildings I remember best from my young days. Grady's is still there, but the church is now an empty shell.

I don't know exactly know how or when I showed up in Webb's Bend, or even in the Cherokee Nation part of the Indian Territory for that matter. Though I've tried, I simply cannot remember who or where I was before Missus. What I am is also mysterious. I would examine my face in the full-length mirror with the gold carved frame, the one that hung in the hallway of the big house where Missus lived and I looked African, but not all African. I thought I could see some Cherokee in me, too. I was nearly sure of that. It wasn't too surprising. A lot of people were mixed around here in Cherokee country, but people with African blood and brown skin, like mine, were the slaves. There were hundreds and hundreds of slaves, perhaps thousands, working on Cherokee farms and plantations, not just in Webb's Bend, either. On the Vanner plantation, where I lived, there must have been dozens of us, though I never counted the exact number. We did everything on that place. Everything. We worked on the land and worked in the house. We worked building and repairing. We kept animals. We were blacksmiths, cooks, maids, you name it. When a visitor knocked on the front door of the big house, it was an African slave who answered the door and asked you your business on the plantation, questioning who you wanted to see and why. Funny thing was, I knew more about some of the other slaves than I did about my own past. A number of Vanner slaves came along with Mr. Money Joe's father, when he moved from the east to the Indian Territory, but that was just the start. Mr. Money Joe was so rich, he could buy slaves all by himself, as many as he needed. He needed plenty of us and not just for his plantation. He also owned slaves to work on his steamships, that cruised up and down the rivers, moving people and goods.

The big slave owners protected their wealth with strict laws about what slaves couldn't do and the punishment for disobeying, but when the Cherokee Council passed the one about slaves not being taught to read or write, luck was with me. That law came too late to stop me because by then, I was really good at it. I loved reading. There was hardly anything I couldn't or wouldn't read. Books of all kinds, newspapers, magazines, maps, anything in the big house with words on it, I'd read. I'm not saying I understood it all. Missus could answer some of my questions, early on. As I my questions became more sophisticated, more challenging to her, she wouldn't even respond. I stopped asking. I didn't want to embarrass her or make her mad. I don't know exactly how old I was then. I don't know how old I am now for that matter. I truly do not know my birthday to this day, or even the year of my birth. There are some records of Cherokee slave births, but not mine. Around the time my 1842 story begins, Missus thought I could be tall for fourteen years old, or, then again, I might be sixteen. Depending on how I felt any given day, I thought of myself as any teen year that suited me. That was good enough, because there were lots of slaves who didn't know how old they were either. Still, I wondered about my natural parents. If I walked down the street and my mother saw me, would she know me? Did I look like my father? Brothers? Sisters? They remained nothing but questions. Everybody I knew on the plantation had an opinion about my stock and saw almost everything in me. Some said, "Book Boy looks all African." Some said, "Book Boy looks half African, half Cherokee." Some said, "Book Boy looks half African, half white." Some said, "Book Boy looks African, Cherokee and white." All the guessing would have been kind of funny, except for the fact that I really did want to know who my parents were. Not because I cared at all what part of what race I was. I wanted to know who I was, not what I was. I was a little jealous that there were other slaves who at least knew who their mother was. Knowing your father was a little harder. I didn't know either one.

Folks used to talk about the special treatment Missus gave me and guessed, like I did, that I must be related to her. I tried my best to figure it out but I never could. I would roll it over in my mind again and again. I kept coming back to Mr. Money Joe. He hardly paid me any attention. If he were my father wouldn't he at least want to talk to me a little? Yet he didn't stop Missus from teaching me to read and write. That was odd. And every day I heard him yelling at the other slaves around my age to go help out in the fields and quit being lazy. Me, he left pretty much to myself. Did he tell Missus to be good to me and teach me? Was Mr. Money Joe my father and just didn't want to say? Naturally, I could never ask him, or Missus. No matter how kind she was, I was still just a slave boy on her plantation. I always knew that there was a permanent, if sometimes invisible line that separated slave from free, even when they were close and occasionally friendly, as I was with Missus. I always had to be aware that she was my owner and I was her slave.

Missus and Mr. Money Joe went to church sometimes. They made it known that they were Christians, but they never did want to be baptized, and I saw enough of the old Cherokee religion in their house that said otherwise. Like so much that happened around Webb's Bend, the Vanners' religion was like a mix of stuff in a great, big stew pot. Which way the stew came out depended on what flavor you were in the mood for that day. It wasn't hard to figure out that them going to church on Sunday was more of a way to meet up with other plantation owners than anything else, and so, at least on Sunday mornings, they were Christians. Some of the other Cherokees seemed to be believers during the service and maybe they were. Come Sunday afternoon, when the service was over, who knows? The Vanners didn't mind if their slaves went to church on Sunday mornings, but it generally wasn't the same church they went to. They went to Reverend Parker's Baptist church and we went to Reverend Watson's Baptist church. Reverend Watson was a well-mannered, kindly man who smiled a lot. Not too tall and kind of round, Reverend Watson happily welcomed everyone to the church and had no problem including slaves. Whenever he had the notion, he liked coming around to neighborhood kitchens for pie and coffee, courtesy of the congregants, but there was nothing he liked better than baptizing a new convert in the creek near the church. People called it Conversion Creek. He would be all smiles as he ducked them in the water and blessed them. I think that's why he was sent to Webb's Bend from up north, to convert as many Cherokees and African slaves as he could.

In truth, a lot of the slaves found much in his religion to like. It went straight to the heart when he talked about God loving everybody just the same, from Mr. Money Joe right on down to the slaves who worked for him, everybody equal, everybody just the same. And then there was the question of freedom. The preacher talked a lot about how God wanted every person to be free. He would never come right out and say that God was against slavery. He didn't have to, because we all knew what he meant, just as we all knew that if he ever did speak directly against slavery, it would spell the end of our church. This was a touchy subject not only for the slave owners, who would never allow a preacher to loosen the iron grip they held on their property, but because the Cherokees themselves were divided on the question. Most Cherokees didn't own slaves and, occasionally, you could hear someone speak openly in opposition to it, at the risk of making his rich kin angry. That was rare. Of course, the rich Cherokees couldn't imagine not having slaves to work the land, cook for them, clean for them, build their houses. What the master required, the slaves would see to. We didn't necessarily like doing it, but we did it anyhow. That's the way it was. A slave does what the master says or he's punished. It was the threat of punishment more than anything else that kept a slave in his place. The slave could be hurt, maybe seriously, even killed, and there was no protection, no judge to appeal to.

At first, Reverend Watson had the only church in town and when he delivered those sermons about how God loved everyone the same, they grumbled about slavery even more. Then we found out there was more than one kind of Baptist Minister. Reverend Parker appeared, sent from back east,

Georgia, I think. He came with enough money to start another church in Webb's Bend and the rich Cherokees, like the Vanners, used to go to that church. From what I could tell, most of what Reverend Parker said was very like Reverend Watson, except he made it clear that God gave full permission for people to own slaves. In fact, he said, a man could own as many slaves as he wanted and it was just fine with God. As a boy, this always confused me. Here, they were both Baptists. They were both Ministers. They both believed in the same God and the same Bible. So how could one say I should be free and the other one say I should be a slave? I wasn't the only one confused, either. Fairness was important to Cherokees. I remember how they got pretty angry when it came out that the Government Agent was stealing their money, money that was supposed to be part of the deal they made to come to the Indian Territory in the first place. People used to come to the Vanner house to talk about it and I heard enough to know they thought they were being cheated. I used to say to myself, at least they know who their parents are. At least they are free to come and go as they please. But I guess nobody likes to feel cheated, even free folks.

Mr. Money Joe and the other slave owners would also complain about Reverend Watson and the other abolition preachers in the Territory who, they said, were stirring up all kinds of trouble. They blamed almost everything that went wrong with slaves on the abolition preachers. We slaves knew better, though. Even if there were no such thing as an abolition preacher, we just did not want to be slaves, that's all. Not really much of a mystery. At one meeting I overheard, the slave owners were upset when one or two tried to run away. It went deeper than just losing their property, as they put it. They were downright scared of those slaves. They feared that the slaves were going to take revenge on them and their families, killing them in their sleep or something like that. Also, if they let slaves get away with running, the whole thing could fall apart. They wouldn't be able to lead their rich, easy lives anymore. When things like that happened, they clamped down hard. That's probably when they made the rule that you couldn't teach a slave to read or write. They didn't want slaves to know anything more than what they needed to know in order to do their work.

I was lucky that Missus taught me before they made that law against reading. After the law, since Missus was a Cherokee, she would surely be punished, maybe have to pay some money to the council or something like that. If Reverend Watson, who was not a Cherokee, tried to teach us how to read the Bible, or teach us to read a hymn to sing in church, or a prayer, they would run him right out of Cherokee land. Believe me, he'd be happy to get out without something else much worse happening to him. I think the worst law was that if a slave tried to defend himself when a free person beat him or lashed him for any reason, that free person could just kill the slave right on the spot, no questions. It was the free person's right to do it. That was the Cherokee Nation law and the masters never let us forget it. So, maybe they were right to be afraid of us reading. Reading could make us feel even more like we want to be free. Also, the newspapers I found in Missus's house talked about people who didn't like slavery. I only knew that they existed because I could read.

In one way, slavery made things pretty easy for those rich ones. But, in another way, if the slave owners were always worried that to keep their fortunes they also had to keep a strong grip on the lives of so many people, it could be a tense and difficult existence. They might be worried that those enslaved people would continually try to run away. They might be afraid that they would hold a grudge and try to hurt their owners, hurt their families, or their farms because of the punishments they received. Yes, these slaves might even care to see their owners dead, more than they cared for their own lives as slaves. I suppose all that could be very tough on the nerves. They had to hire men called overseers, to make sure we did as we were told and to deal with us if we didn't. They had to hire slave catchers to bring back the ones who ran for freedom.

I hated being a slave. I did what I was told only because I was afraid of what would happen to me if I didn't. I thought a lot about what it must be like to be free, to be able to say, "No. I don't want to do that. I'm not going to do what you want me to do, because I'm going to do what I want to do and go where I want to go." That would be pure happiness, I thought. It's not that I didn't like Missus. I did, very much, but there's not enough liking in the whole world that would make me choose to be anybody's slave, even Missus.

There was one thing they couldn't own, not even with all their whips and guns. They couldn't own your thoughts. The masters couldn't stop you from thinking and that was big for me. The preachers said each person had their own soul, on the inside, that belonged only to them and God. You couldn't see it, but it was there and it was yours. I wasn't completely sure what that meant, but I did think it was a good thing, because I liked that there was an inside part of me that slave masters couldn't touch. I would play a game that I was free, inside. I might not be free on the plantation, but I played a quiet game to myself that I was free in my mind and I could let myself think anything I wanted to think. I called it the freedom game. The freedom game kept me going more times than I want to remember now. As I look back, I can remember that, when I would play the freedom game, I would usually be thinking about some place or about doing something I had read about. In my thoughts, I was reading my own book, one in which slavery didn't exist. Sometimes I would get to feeling all knotted up inside and the world would start spinning around. I would get so dizzy I thought I might fall down. I could feel my heart pounding, like it wasn't even inside my body, it was so strong. I could hear the pounding in my ears, too. I felt like I was going to die right there on the spot. I wanted to run, someplace, any place, but I knew I couldn't and besides my feet wouldn't move. I thought: this is what it is to be crazy. I didn't see how I could live much longer. Then I would get myself to play the freedom game. You see, in the game, I could go anywhere. In the game I could do anything I wanted because it was in my head, in my mind. Sure, I knew it was just a game, but I could make it feel real. The more details I made up about where I was going or what I was doing, the deeper into the game I went. All of a sudden, my heart slowed down and I felt like me again. Playing the game gave me a way out of those knots in my stomach and the spinning in my head. I wasn't going to die after all. I felt better. The game worked. That kind of thing didn't happen very often, but when it did happen, I was thankful for having the freedom game.

I figured, why just play the freedom game when I felt bad? I could also play the freedom game to have some fun, too. Say, I was doing some kind of boring, uncomfortable chore, like pulling weeds out of Missus's vegetable garden in the hot sun. Secretly, I would dream something up, something fun and exciting. Maybe I would pretend I was on a huge ship out on the big sea. I had to imagine what the sea smelled like because I'd never actually been to the sea. I used to read about the sea, though, and the ships and the sailors in some of Missus's books. There were two in particular that stuck with me. One was about pirates and sword fights. They were always fighting about something, usually gold and women. The other one was about the British Navy. I learned later on it was the very same Britain that we fought to be our own country. According to the book, the British were great sailors, so it made me proud that we beat them in a war. I didn't think like that then, though. I didn't really feel like I was a part of America until Mr. Lincoln won the War Between the States. In those days of slavery, I needed the freedom game to feel like a part of anything.

CHAPTER 2

Not all Cherokee people were of one mind when it came to slavery. Most did not own slaves themselves. Some owned one or two. The great numbers of us were owned by wealthy plantation families and they kept our numbers growing. They had hundreds and hundreds of slaves then and by the time the War Between the States broke out, maybe thousands. Of all the Cherokees I knew who were opposed to slavery in Webb's Bend, Jumping Ben and Miss Annie were the most certain that slavery was wrong, but even they cautiously kept this views to themselves and close friends. I had overheard Ben talking about it in a very private conversation that took place in the most central place in Webb's Bend, Grady's General Store. There wasn't much to the main street in the town. For me, Grady's General Store was the best of it. They sold everything you could need, at least I thought so then. They had bolts of cloth with the needles and thread to turn the cloth into clothes and curtains and such. There was writing paper, pen and ink, a few books and magazines, and a post office to mail what you wrote. They had hardware goods like iron nails, saws and hammers. There were plates and dishes, flints, powder, balls and muskets. And let's not forget the sweets. They had hard candies from the east that I used to sneak from Missus's desk. That's where she kept her candies, right next to her tobacco pouch and smoking pipe. She thought it was a secret place, but I knew just where to go for a treat. I was on an errand for Missus at Grady's, collecting a parcel that had arrived by mail, when I overheard the conversation. I walked up to the counter and announced that I was there for Missus's parcel, having been told it was waiting for her. Roger Ficklin, the clerk, told me he'd get it in a minute. He knew who I was and that I ran errands for Missus, but he never liked or trusted me. So, I sat and waited for the parcel on an empty wooden crate in the back of the store, bored, as I knew I would be last on his list. It was a pretty big store and from where I sat, I was not easily seen, but I could hear everything

THE FREEDOM GAME

clearly and it turned out to be quite an interesting talk, at that. Jumping Ben, Ficklin, and a man called Yellow Tree, all Cherokees who lived in Webb's Bend, were talking. It seems Yellow Tree had recently been told that he had lost his job as the blacksmith on the William plantation. A slave was now doing the work that Yellow Tree had been paid wages to do for several years. That job was his only source of money and he was running out of his savings, fast.

"I'm almost at the bottom of my money box, Roger," Yellow Tree said in a raised voice to the store clerk. "I just can't afford to pay what you are asking for this length of rope." He held up a coil of rope. "I might as well go out and get myself hung and get the rope for free." He stuck his tongue out as though he were being strangled by a rope. The three men all laughed, but Jumping Ben turned serious quickly.

"That slave, I think his name is Matthew... he's doing your work now, right?" Ben placed his hand on Yellow Tree's shoulder. Yellow Tree solemnly nodded yes. Ben continued, "And you trained him, right? Taught him every-thing he knows about blacksmithing?" Again, Yellow Tree nodded, agreeing with what Ben was saying. Ben shook his head in disapproval. "Well, I just don't think it's the way things should be. No sir. A Cherokee blacksmith, or a Cherokee carpenter, or anybody should be able to work his trade in his own town and get paid for it. And shouldn't have himself kicked out of his job and be replaced with an unpaid slave; a slave who he himself taught from his own good work and skillful knowledge. I got nothing against Matthew. I'm sure an he's okay man, but you tell me why he should be a slave in the first place? Who says a man can own another man? Why do we need slaves here in Webb's Bend in the first place, huh? The whole thing is just plain wrong." Ficklin nervously looked out of the window. Ben pointed to me, evidently aware that I had been listening to the entire discussion. "Take Book Boy over there." He beckoned to me with his hand. "Come here, Book Boy."

"Yes, sir." I obediently hurried to where they were standing by the counter.

"You came here on an errand for the Vanners?" I nodded. "Did they pay you?" I shook my head 'no.' "But you're a smart boy, aren't you? Could be the smartest boy in Webb's Bend. And yet they pay you nothing for your good work. Do you wish you could have a job to earn money and go where you please, when you please?" I stood silently, afraid to answer that I ached

15

to be free. Slaves had been severely punished for less. Jumping Ben smiled. "That's alright, Book Boy, you don't need to say a word. I already know your answer."

" I should leave Webb's Bend, my friend," Yellow Tree said. "I lived here a long time, but maybe I've got to move on and try blacksmithing someplace where they don't have a slave to do it for free. Someplace where they don't have slaves at all and people can do the work they're meant to do."

Ficklin leaned forward with his hands on the counter. "Well, your someplace might be wherever that Reverend Watson came from," he said. "That man preaches about slavery just as much as he preaches about the Bible. Maybe more. Ben, you ever been to his church? He sure gets everybody all worked up about it. I'm surprised the Light-horse haven't moved him and his church a long way out of this town. Or made him disappear altogether, if you know what I mean."

Ben stroked his face, thinking. "No, Roger, I haven't ever been. I'm not one for church, Watson's or the other one. Never been baptized, either. Didn't care to. I like the old religion. It makes more sense to me. Not that they haven't tried to get me to do it. I can hardly walk down the road in front of a church without the Minister running after me to come in and talk about the Bible." He laughed. "They run after me halfway down the street, promising to give me coffee and sweets if I come to the church. I like coffee and sweets, but to me it's not worth having to listen to their talk. A couple of minutes and I'm ready to go on my way. I will say that I do agree about the slaves, though. People should be free to do and go and be what they want. It's a shame what they do to the Africans. A shame. And look where it leaves old Yellow Tree here. I'm okay, because Annie and I live off the land. We grow what we need, we hunt meat in the woods, we eat fish from the river. We have what we need from the land. That's good for me and it's enough. What about the folks like old Yellow Tree? Every year there are more and more slaves, which means less and less work for Cherokees. People are already so poor they don't know what to do to live from day to day. I'm talking too much, I know. But I have to say it's a shame. A shame."

Yellow Tree put the palm of his hand on his chest. Then he pointed to Jumping Ben. "Thank you, my friend. Thank you for understanding my trouble. I'm not the hunter you are. I'm not the fisherman you are. I'm not the farmer your Annie is. I only know one thing, to blacksmith. And I'm a good blacksmith, too. I must leave my friends to find a town that needs a person like me. I think that's a town with no slaves. I am sad to go."

This kind of talk made Ficklin afraid. He was worried that someone would hear their conversation. The store was owned by a rich slave master, and he thought that if the talk got back to him, Yellow Tree wouldn't be the only Cherokee to lose his job that week. He looked out the window again to see if anyone outside had been listening. Then he looked straight at me. "Hey, Book Boy. What are you doing here?"

"Waiting for Missus's parcel, sir."

"Here, boy," Ficklin said gruffly and reached under the counter and took out a package. He examined the writing on it. "Come here, I said."

"Yes sir." I ran to the counter.

He handed me the parcel but held his had on top so I couldn't take it just yet. The store clerk said in a low, threatening voice, "You hear anything in this store today, boy? Anything at all?"

"No sir. I was thinking about something else the whole time." I was lying and he knew it. I heard every word and I was proud of Jumping Ben.

"You know what I would do to you if you told somebody, anybody about this conversation?" Just then Jumping Ben broke in, coming to my defense.

Ben smiled and said, "Book Boy is okay. You're okay, aren't you Book Boy?" He gave me a reassuring pat on the arm. "You wouldn't want to cause Mr. Ficklin any trouble, would you?"

"No, Mr. Ben, I never would. No Mr. Ficklin, I never would," I said in an overly truthful way.

Roger Ficklin took his hand off of the package. "Go on, then. Go on. And don't you forget what I told you," he snarled.

I ran out of the store, clutching the package close to my chest with both arms, glad to be leaving. I was trying to digest what I had heard. Slavery was complicated for the Cherokees. One thing was clear to me, though. Jumping Ben wished there was no slavery. And it wasn't only on account of his black-smith friend losing his job. I could see that he also believed it was wrong for one person to take the freedom of another person.

It made me think that there must be other Cherokees who believed slavery to be wrong, but were unwilling to admit it openly. I could understand that. Most people wouldn't want the trouble that would come down on them if they were heard talking that way. Poor Ficklin was scared to death without anybody listening, and he hadn't even said much of anything himself. Slavery had all of us, slave and free, tangled up in a sticky web we just couldn't get out of. Slavery enslaved everybody. If you were free, maybe you earned your living from working in a trade on the plantations, or you sold them something to earn your money. And if you spoke against slavery, they might not buy from you or do business with you anymore. They might even come after you to shut you up or run you out. Of course, slaves themselves would never dare to speak out against it, even in the church of an abolitionist preacher like Reverend Watson. A slave was somebody's property and the master could do anything he wanted to do with that property. I wasn't the only slave boy who couldn't figure who my pa was. It was well known that some masters would bring a slave girl to the bed when they wanted.

Jumping Ben liked that I could read, even though he was a Cherokee and knew the law against it. He never learned to read himself, but sometimes he would come across a book or a magazine and bring it home. He would thumb through the whole thing, carefully studying all the pictures and trying to make out some letters and a few familiar words. Looking at the pictures would get him only so far, though. Ben wanted to know what the words said, and what the pictures meant. When he got hold of an interesting book, he would come looking for me, to ask if I would read it to him. If I was able to slip away, I was happy to do it and his wife Miss Annie would give me something sweet for my trouble. Since I was always running errands for Missus, nobody gave me a second look if I walked off, as long as I was back where I was supposed to be in time. Ben and Miss Annie lived in a one room wood house by the river. They would take out the thing they wanted me to read, sit themselves down, one on the bed and one on the only chair they owned. There they sat until it was finished. I sat on the dirt floor. They had a shed with no windows in back of the house. That's where Ben kept his tools and such. He was a pretty good carpenter. If I got tired or just wanted to be alone, they would let me lie down in the shed for a while. I liked them a lot and they liked me. Even though they were free Cherokees and I was a slave, I knew we were friends.

One time, Ben asked me to read a letter that came from Miss Annie's sister. She lived in Texas. "Hey Book Boy. How about coming to the house

THE FREEDOM GAME

later? Miss Annie got a letter from her sister and she's itching to find out what it says. She hasn't seen her sister in a real long time, ever since she moved to Texas with her husband and their children. Annie's been feeling a little down lately and it would be good for her to have the news. What do you say? I'll bet there's a sweet, crunchy cookie in it for you."

This sounded interesting. A letter from a whole other country, Texas. "Sure thing, Ben. I'll be by this afternoon, as soon as I finish for Missus."

Later that day, Jumping Ben and Miss Annie sat and listened as I stood before them in their cabin, reading. I wasn't exactly sure where Texas was, but from the letter, it sounded like kind of a rough place. Miss Annie's sister talked about how she was afraid that fighting with the Mexicans could start again at any time. She said Mexico had many more people than Texas, so it had a bigger army, with cannons and cavalry. She also said the living was hard and they didn't have many slaves to help where she lived. The ones they did have would sometimes try to run away to Mexico because you couldn't own slaves there. I remember her exact words were, "It's hard to keep a slave where we live because the Mexico border is so close, a slave might just pick up and run there, free as a bird and never come back." When I read those glorious words out loud, I they bounced off the cabin walls and came straight back at me, like I was hit by lightning. They echoed in my head, "...free as a bird and never come back." I will never forget that letter. I tried to hide my excitement from Ben and Miss Millie. I knew what Ben thought about slavery, but didn't know how they would feel about me wanting so much to be free. I never told them about the freedom game or anything like that. We didn't talk about things like that. I tried my best to keep on reading, as if nothing special happened. I couldn't tell you what the rest of the letter said, though. All I thought about was this place called Mexico, so close, a slave in Texas could be free as a bird. The freedom game started to feel more and more real. I pictured myself as that bird, an eagle. I was an eagle, flying to Mexico, flying to my freedom. All on the inside, of course. I dared not say a single word about Mexico to anyone.

Yes, Jumping Ben and Miss Annie were my friends, but my best friend in world was Caleb. He was strong and smart and much older than me. He could cipher numbers faster than anyone, faster even than me and I was fast. Many times, Caleb was put in charge of special jobs because he figured out how to do it, he could pick the right men to do the work, the right materials

19

and the right tools. He told me once that Mr. Money Joe bought him at top dollar from a Cherokee farmer because of his skills and honesty. He helped build some of the important Cherokee places and was quick to see which slaves could do what kind of work well. Mr. Money Joe would hire him out to other Cherokees for a big fee. He could be depended on to go to the workplace, do the job and return to the Vanner plantation when the day's work was done. Caleb was a real money-maker for the Vanners. He was hired out so much, Mr. Money Joe reckoned that he needed his own horse to get wherever he was working on time. Caleb loved that horse. He called her Bandana since she had a dark brown patch around the neck, which showed up sort of like a bandana against her lighter colored body. Caleb wouldn't let anybody else ride Bandana and he was the only one to feed her, water her and groom her. Bandana was a good horse and Caleb took especially good care of her. Bandana was the only thing in this world Caleb could really call his own.

The idea that Bandana belonged to Caleb seemed acceptable because Caleb helped build Reverend Watson's church. At first it was because Mr. Money Joe hired him out to do the work, but as Caleb got to know Reverend Watson and heard more of his views about slavery, he kept staying later and later, working on the building even after the other slaves were gone. Reverend Watson treated Caleb better than he was treated on any other job he was hired out to do. He would bring Caleb water and food at midday. He would sit with Caleb as he ate and would talk about what it was like where he came from and how all people are equal in the sight of God. Caleb wasn't ready to be baptized, but he did like the sound of that and appreciated the Reverend's friendly ways. He thought of Reverend Watson as a good man and sincere in his beliefs. Caleb ended up building most of that church himself and he took special care to make it a fine building. When it was finished and everyone in Webb's Bend was invited to the first service, from the pulpit, Reverend Watson made it a point to thank Caleb for his "splendid work." He said, "Surely the Lord has guided the hands of this wonderful man, to complete such a magnificent structure as we now have for our prayers." Caleb didn't know what magnificent meant, but he did know he was called a man by the preacher, not a slave. The important difference between those two words was not lost on Caleb. He was proud of himself and the work he did building that church. So was the congregation that grew quickly, mostly from slaves joining in the service. The Church benches that Caleb built were filled on Sundays. The congregation was happy to forget their troubles for a little while to pray, sing and hear from a preacher who wanted them to be free. Among them were a number of true believers who asked to be baptized into the Baptist faith of Reverend Watson and were accepted happily. The slaves of Webb's Bend loved the church that Caleb built. It made his name known even to slaves from other farms and plantations. Even after the work was completed, he remained a personal favorite of Reverend Watson.

Caleb was especially popular among the Vanner slaves. They looked up to him, not only for his skill and knowledge, but also his judgment. If, as often happened, there was a dispute between slaves, the people involved would bring the problem to him and if they didn't come to him on their own, then people close to them might come to Caleb for advice on handling the delicate matter. I learned why people trusted him when I, myself, needed his help with a problem. There was a magazine missing from the Grady's general store book shelf. It was the newest issue of the Ladies' Companion, the newest issue in Webb's Bend, that is. Ladies' Companion was a great magazine full of news and poems and artwork. I didn't care that it said Ladies' on the cover, I would read Missus's copy from front to back whenever she brought one home. When the Grady's clerk, Roger Ficklin, reported it missing, I was the first, and only, one he suspected. In fact, he told Missus that I was the one who stole the magazine. He was sure. He had not seen me take it with his own eyes, but he was still sure that I was the thief. First, I was in the store all the time. Second, I was a slave and he didn't trust slaves, ever. Third, and most important, I was the only slave in Webb's Bend who could read. To him, that was clear proof I was guilty. A slave who can read would surely be right at the top of his list of suspects for almost anything and especially for a stolen magazine. To his thinking, what other slave would even be interested in having it, and since all slaves were natural thieves... well, the mystery, for him, was solved. His problem was that he knew Missus owned me and she was a powerful lady. She trusted me with errands and he knew that, too. He couldn't just go off and give me a beating like he would any other slave boy accused of stealing. He would have to go to Missus and get her permission to beat me.

I was scared. A slave's word against a Cherokee's word was not even a contest. The slave would always be thought of as lying. Even if the whole world knew it was the Cherokee lying, the slave would be blamed. That's how it was and I had no chance. I was going to get a beating and there was nothing I could do about it. To add to my trouble, they would expect me to return the magazine, even though I had no magazine to return. It was a rainy fall day, but I was sweating. When Roger Ficklin came around to the Vanner place to talk to Missus one afternoon, it was to tell Missus that I was a thief. Sure enough, Rose, a slave in the big house who looked after me, had overheard what they were talking about. She told me to keep from being seen until Ficklin had gone. I hid behind my favorite tree and waited and waited and waited for what seemed like half the day. I think Missus put him off, though, because after he finally left, she sent Rose to tell me that she wanted to talk to me first thing in the morning. Rose said she did not look very happy. That she didn't beat me herself in front of Roger Ficklin meant that she didn't really believe I did it. Whether or not Missus believed the Grady's clerk, she would still have to satisfy him somehow and she was putting it off until tomorrow. I felt the panic rising inside me. It was supper time, but I didn't feel like eating. Rose tried to get me to eat something, but I was too upset, thinking about the beating I would get tomorrow. And what if beating was not enough punishment for them? What if they wanted to make an example out of me to teach the other slaves never to steal? Would I get the lash? Would they hang me from a limb of my favorite tree? These thoughts raced around my mind over and over. Even the freedom game didn't help me. This time I couldn't put my mind on it. I couldn't think of anything but the terrible tomorrow that waited for me.

I decided to lie down. My sleeping place was a spot on the floor of the east slave house. It was not yet time to sleep and I was alone in the dim room. As I stepped over bundles of clothing and slaves' personal items, making my way to my spot in the corner, something unusual caught my eye. A girl named Misty had recently been assigned to sleep in the east slave house and her blanket roll lay open in the middle of the floor. She was new to the Vanner plantation. The kitchen staff had lost a girl who died from the milk sickness, so Missus bought her from another Cherokee plantation. Misty was around my age. Already, she had the look of a beautiful woman, but a young, playful way about her. She was funny and she liked to imitate the older slaves, the way they gave orders or the way they walked or ate. She made me laugh because she really could make herself look and sound like them acting silly. Misty hated that some of the older slaves treated us much the same as our Cherokee masters did, as though they owned us, too. I could tell by watching her that she wanted so much to be free, to have pretty clothes and go to far away places. I liked her a lot, but I didn't tell her about the freedom game. I was afraid she would think I was crazy. Besides, hearing her talk in such detail about what she wanted, she might have been playing her own freedom game already. I figured someday I would probably tell her all about it. At that moment, I was standing over her stuff in the slave house. A plain kitchen slave dress was laid flat on her floor spot, but in the middle of the clothing, I could just barely make out the outline of something with four corners, inside the dress. What kind of cloth would make a shape like that, I wondered? I bent down and looked closer. There was definitely something inside the dress. I looked around to see if anyone had entered the one-room house while I knelt in front of Misty's spot. I was still alone. I carefully lifted the hem and slid my hand underneath, between the layers of dress, to feel around for what was in there. I touched something. It felt like paper. I gently pulled it out, trying not to disturb the flat dress. I read the cover, whispering to myself, "The Ladies' Companion." I was shocked. Misty was the thief!

I felt such a mixture of emotions. I liked Misty. I considered her a friend. There weren't too many slaves around my age at the Vanner place. It was more fun when she came to work here. I would think about her sometimes. Really, I thought about her a lot. She was pretty, but also there was something about the way one eyebrow would go up when she looked at me that I just couldn't get out of my mind. I think she enjoyed talking to me, too. There was definitely something between us and whatever it was, I didn't want it to stop. Finding the stolen magazine in her things was disappointing to me because I thought she was a good, honest person. If I told Missus, Misty would be punished, maybe beaten, maybe sold. I hated the thought of her being hurt. Even worse was the thought that I might never see her again. Of course, she would hate me forever if I said anything. Maybe that was the worst of all. I could almost understand why she would take the magazine. A girl like Misty needs to be able to at least look at pretty clothes and dream about being a fancy lady, like the ones in the magazine's pictures. Having that magazine to look at maybe relieved the sting of being a slave a little, taking orders all day from everyone around her, even other slaves, with no life of her own. It was wrong to steal, though. Everybody knows that. But, she certainly couldn't buy it for herself. Slaves had no money and, by law, couldn't own anything anyway, even if she could buy it. The only way for her to have that magazine was to steal it or be given it by Roger Ficklin. What she would have to do for him to receive it as a gift would be far more terrible than stealing it, so that was out of the question. That left stealing as the only way for her to look at the magazine. I was beginning to forgive her for stealing it, knowing in my heart that stealing was wrong. She should not have done it and I was angry that she had. I was also sorry for her that this one small pleasure could only be had by becoming a thief. Then, there was the position she had put me in. I was the accused. This was the most confused I had ever been. I truly did not know what to do. I had to do something. I needed to talk to someone wiser than me, someone whom I could trust with these fearful secrets. Lucky for me, there was someone like that. Caleb was the one to see. He and I had talked over a lot of things over the years I had known him. He was smart and careful in what he said. He wanted the best for me, I know. Like many other slaves, I found him to be a fair and honest judge. He had so much experience and a desire for the right side to win in the end. Caleb was definitely the one to see for help.

As quietly as I could, I slipped the magazine back into Misty's dress, just the way I had found it. I peeked out of the window, and making sure I was still alone and no one would see me, I left the slave house and went to look for Caleb. I somehow had the impression that I was already betraying Misty simply by looking through her things. It was odd, because I was really the one in trouble here, not her, at least not yet. It was getting darker and cooler by the minute which made what I had done seem that much more like spying on her. Instead of the coming punishment that I had been dreading, Misty had strangely become the center of my thoughts. Protecting Misty was what I wanted above anything. I couldn't put my finger on why that was happening, but, nevertheless, it was. It's true that I cared about other people. I didn't ever want to see someone hurt or sick. This was different. This was the first time I had ever been willing to put another person's happiness before my own. I couldn't explain it to myself. Maybe Caleb could.

I found Caleb enjoying the early evening air sitting comfortably with his back to a wide tree. He was humming a favorite song that I'd heard him sing before. He worked hard most days and in the evening he needed to relax. That's what gave him the strength to put in another day's hard work. Caleb used to say, "This body is like a tick tock clock. If you don't take the time to re-wind it up, the clock will have no time left for you."

"Hey Caleb. You got a minute to talk?" I said. I must have looked a little shaky. He saw right off that something was wrong.

"Of course. Of course. Set your self down right over here, boy." He patted the ground next to him by the tree. "Some trouble, huh?" I sat down next to him. "Well maybe if you talk it over with old Caleb, we can figure what to do." He rubbed my head and gave me a warm smile. It was almost like giving me permission to cry. I didn't realize I had so much feeling about this until then. I didn't let myself completely cry, but he noticed a few tears streaming down my face. "That's alright, son. Don't you worry. Whatever it is, we'll find the answer. Anything can be fixed."

I sniffed it down and wiped my eyes fast, hoping he hadn't seen the tears, though I knew he had. "Well, I'm in a real bad situation, Caleb. See, Roger Ficklin, he's the clerk at Grady's General Store, came to see Missus today. He told her that he's sure I took something from the store without paying for it. He told her I was a thief." I got very defensive, raising my voice. "I never stole anything from anybody in my whole life and that's the truth!" I looked around to see if anyone had heard my outburst.

"I know you didn't, son. I know. What did he say you took?"

"A magazine called 'The Ladies' Companion'," I told him. "He said all slaves steal and since I'm the only slave he knows in Webb's Bend who can read, I must have been the one who stole it. But I didn't. I swear."

"I believe you, Book Boy. The trick," he said, "is in getting Missus and the clerk to believe you, too. Let's think on this for a minute." He pulled a tall blade of grass and put it in the corner of his mouth, playing with it between his fingers. "Half of making it right is giving the stolen thing back, but if you didn't take it, then you don't have it to give back, so that's a problem. Besides, maybe the fool clerk lost it or stole it himself and just wants to put the blame to someone else. Not uncommon. And a slave boy is easy to blame."

"No, that's not it. It was stolen. That's a fact."

"Truly? How can you be so sure?" he said still calmly playing with the blade of grass. My face was hot and flushed, knowing that I was about to give away Misty's secret, a secret she had no idea I even knew. I must have been too quiet and I probably looked odd because Caleb turned to see me square in my face. "You know who took it, don't you, son?"

"Yes sir, I do," I whispered.

"Well come on, then. Let's have it."

"It was Misty." I put my hand over my eyes, not quite believing what I had just done.

"Ohhh. You mean that pretty little house slave you been hanging around every chance you get?" Caleb chuckled. "Now I get it." He turned serious. "And you want to protect her, don't you? You're alright, Book Boy. You're a good man." He slapped me on the leg. I think he was proud of me. I started feeling better, more sure of myself. He leaned over toward me. "Tell me this, how can you be so sure she's the one who took it?"

"I found it under her dress."

He gave me an exaggerated look of surprise with extra wide eyes and then laughed out loud, "And what was your hand doing under there, my young friend!"

I answered so fast, I was tripping over my own words, "What? No! It wasn't like that! No! I didn't have my hand under her dress. Well I did, but it was more up, no, between. No! She wasn't wearing the dress. I mean when my hand was in it." I just put my head in my hands as Caleb laughed so hard he could barely breathe. This time I spoke slowly and carefully, "Alright. Here's what happened. I was alone in the slave house. I saw the outline of the magazine hidden in her dress on the floor. I slid my hand in and took out the magazine to be sure. Then I put it back the same way I found it."

Caleb stopped laughing. "I see. That's where it is now?"

"Yes. And Ficklin the clerk is coming back tomorrow to find out how I'm going to be punished. They're going to lash me for sure."

"You won't tell them who stole it, will you?" he asked, already knowing my answer.

"Never. Not if they lashed me a hundred times. Two hundred times. Not if they..."

Caleb held up his hand to stop me. "I get it. Alright. I get it." He paused for a bit and then asked, "Missus ever send you to buy one of these magazines before?"

"All the time. She's got a big stack of them. I like to read them when she's not around."

Caleb tossed the blade of grass away and leaned in, toward me so no one would hear. "Here's what you do. You take the magazine from Misty's dress, again. This time, you put it on top of Missus's stack of magazines in the big house, without anybody seeing you. When they call you in tomorrow, you say you got it for Missus. You show them the stack. You say that you must have forgotten to put it on her account, so that's why the clerk didn't know. You're sorry if it caused any trouble."

I just stared at him for a minute, letting it sink in. Then the words burst out of my mouth. "That's it! That's brilliant! Brilliant! Thank you, Caleb, thank you!" I could hardly keep from jumping up and down. "It will work. It will work! I know it will."

I slipped back to the slave house. I only had a few minutes before the others would start trickling in to go to sleep. I quickly found the magazine and hid it under my shirt. I ran to the big house. There were two ways in: the front door, where a slave would ask me why I was there, and the back door used by slaves and kitchen deliveries. I chose the back door, even though it meant I would have to pass through the entire first floor to get to Missus's business room where she had her desk and kept her writing things. That's where she would be seeing Roger Ficklin and that's also where her magazines were stacked. First, I had to get through the kitchen.

Misty just popped up out of nowhere. "Hey, Book. What are you up to in the big house tonight? Isn't it kind of late for you young man?" I was startled. She giggled.

"Oh, it's you. I... I just forgot something I had to do in Missus's room. Yes, in the room. There. Down the hall. I'll be right back." She looked confused as I brushed past her and ran down the hall to Missus's business room. I knew Misty would follow me so I had to get there first, put the magazine on the stack and then pretend I was doing something else. As she entered the room, I was already taking something from the top of the desk and putting it, unnecessarily, in the drawer. "Okay, that's done!" I said loudly, with a weak smile and a sigh.

"What's done?" Misty asked.

"Nothing. All taken care of. I'll see you later," I said as I rushed out the front door this time, since it was closer for my getaway and no one would question why I was leaving. I gave Misty a quick wave goodbye as I scrambled down the stairs and made for the slave house. I pretended to be asleep when Misty came in. I heard her rustling around, looking for the magazine she was sure should be there somewhere. It wasn't. She was angrily mumbling to herself. Another voice said, "What's the matter with you, girl? Go to sleep." I wanted so much to laugh. I could hardly stop myself from laughing and had to hold my breath a few times when I thought I couldn't contain it. I didn't sleep much that night.

I tried to look as normal as possible the next morning. I went up to the house and made myself look busy when a slave announced that Roger Ficklin had come to see Missus. This was it. I had to be calm and normal. On the inside I was as jittery as a colt, on the outside, calm and normal. Missus called me into her business room where the clerk was waiting to trap me. Missus asked me if I stole something from Grady's, but my mind was spinning. The combination of no sleep and lying to Missus was enough to make me crazy-eyed. I kept telling myself, I can do this, I can do this. I must have been saying it out loud because the clerk came right up to me and looked me in the eye. "What was that, Book Boy?"

"I can...," realizing that I was talking out loud, "I can... show you where I put it."

"Put what, boy?" she said suspiciously.

I don't think she had actually asked me yet. "Oh, what? What... Missus?" I wasn't making any sense, but I didn't know what else to say.

"Book Boy, Mr. Ficklin, here, thinks you stole a magazine from Grady's." She moved Ficklin to the side, to stand right in front of me. "Did you steal it?" she asked, slowly and sternly.

"No, Missus. I didn't steal anything. A magazine? I did bring home the newest Ladies' Companion for you, though."

Roger Ficklin jumped to his feet. "See? I told you he took it!" He pointed his finger at me like he wanted to poke my eye out.

"Uh huh," I said, tilting my head in the direction of the stack, "I put it right over there." All three of us went to the stack and looked at the magazine in question, right on top. "That's it, right?" I asked, innocently. "Did I forget to put it on Missus's account?"

"That's alright, Book Boy. We all make mistakes sometimes. She gave the clerk that look of hers that makes you feel really small. "Don't we, Roger?"

"I sure am sorry if I caused any trouble, Missus," I said, drooping my head.

"You can go now, Book Boy," Missus motioned to the door.

"Yes, Missus." I ran out of that room as fast as I could, out the front door and to the bottom of the steps. I could hear loud talking coming from the house when Misty came running down the stairs. She grabbed my arm and pulled me around to the side of the house where there was no window for someone to see us.

She put her face a couple of inches from mine and looked into my eyes. She whispered, "What did you do? You beautiful boy. You saved me, that's what you did. You put yourself in danger to save me." I could feel her warm moist breath on me. It smelled sweet. I was starting to breathe heavily. She came closer to me. "Book, you're wonderful." Then she put her cheek against my cheek. She was so soft and warm. Her neck smelled sweet, too. Then she put her lips on my lips and kissed me a slow, soft, loving kiss. That was my first kiss, a kiss that took over my whole being, a kiss that I can feel right now like it happened this morning. She gave me another hug, fitting in my arms perfectly. Then, Misty ran back around the corner of the house, looked around and disappeared through the front door. In the space of one day and one night, my life had changed. I found out that I could lie and be believed. I found out that I could keep my head in a rough situation. I found out that I was in love with Misty. I was to find out even more about myself in the days ahead.

CHAPTER 3

Nobody was expecting anything like what was going to happen that sunny November Sunday. Reverend Watson's service hadn't begun, and as usual, everybody was milling around outside, entertaining one another with stories about what happened during the week. I was just listening to whatever I could. After church I always told Missus any good stories going around. She especially seemed to like hearing about what was going on with the slaves' personal lives and would laugh at how silly she thought we were, even if the story was very serious. However, what happened that day was so big, nobody could miss hearing about it. That morning started off in an uneasy way; for some reason we didn't yet know, there were two mounted Light-horse police on the road in front of the church, one tall and muscular, one short, plump and older. I couldn't ever remember seeing any Light-horse even near the church on a Sunday morning before. It was so strange, it felt like something bad was about to happen. Their attention being set on one stretch of road in one direction definitely made it look like they were waiting for someone in particular to show up there. This was mainly a slave church, so I guessed it must be a slave they wanted. It's true that the Light-horsemen enforced all the laws for the Cherokee Nation, but every slave knew that these police also did whatever special enforcing the slave owners needed to have done, or could look the other way, when they were told. It was only natural that people could be heard wondering out loud about why they were there. The two waited and watched intently from atop their mounts. As usual, everyone had made sure to arrive early, ready for the service, but Reverend Watson hadn't opened the door all the way yet for the crowd to come in. He peeked out to see what was happening. I was standing on the church steps and he asked me, "Book Boy, do you know what's going on?"

"Sorry Rev, I'm not sure. But they look like they're waiting for somebody, and they have guns," I answered.

"This is terrible," he said nervously, his voice trembling with concern. "I hope they aren't here to close the church."

"I don't think so, Rev. They would have done it already."

"I suppose you're right, Book Boy."

The congregation continued to enjoy each other's company, joking and gossiping as we waited. The children played on the dry ground, the women dusting them off every few minutes, trying in vain to keep them presentable for the worship to come. For the adults, however, the presence of the Light-horsemen was impossible to ignore. As soon as I spotted Caleb riding in on Bandana, I understood that the police were there on his account. Caleb and Bandana approached the front of the church and those two Light-horsemen made a straight line, right for him, fast. In no time, they were directly in front of him, blocking his movement. Bandana could tell something was wrong. She snorted and kicked the dusty ground, raising a small cloud around all the horses' legs. Bandana's alarm made the other horses jittery, too.

Caleb looked toward the church. I think he was expecting Reverend Watson to help him. That sunny November Sunday, it was wise Caleb, the man who helped everyone, who was in trouble this time, serious trouble. When it was clear they had come to confront Caleb about a police matter, the slaves who had gathered for the service ran over to see what the fuss was about instead. By the time the Reverend opened the door and came out to greet the worshippers, a crowd of about twenty or thirty slaves had encircled Caleb and the Light-horsemen. Mamas hushed their little ones with man slaves, tense and angry, around them. Reverend Watson and everybody strained to see and hear what was going on. The only people who hung back near the church besides the Reverend and me were some slave owners who, surprisingly, had decided to attend our church that day, instead of Reverend Parker's church. They watched with interest, too, but from a good, safe distance, as if they knew trouble was coming. I asked one of them if they knew what was happening. His reply was a word of warning. "If I were you I'd leave this place right now, boy. You don't want to be here today."

"Why not?" I asked.

"Let's just say I know this whole situation is about to get messy. You do as I say and go on home." He glared at me for a bit. I didn't go home. I was interested all the more after what he said. One of the people I held dearest in my life was in some kind of danger. Nothing could tear me from that place.

The Light-horse, still mounted, were in position, now. Caleb couldn't move to the right or the left. The short one spoke first. "Your name is Caleb the slave? From the Vanner place?"

Caleb nodded, saying, "That's me. Yes sir. What..."

"Get off the horse. Now!" he commanded in a very official, business-like way.

Caleb looked confused, trying to stay calm. "Just wait a minute, okay? What'd I do? I'm just going to ..." Before he could finish, they both drew their pistols, pointing them straight at his head. That stopped Caleb from talking. I could see he was shocked but still looked them in the eye. Caleb was not used to this kind of treatment. He was not one to get in trouble. He was never drunk. Never rowdy. Never had cause to be involved with the Light-horse. The crowd moved in a little closer to get a better look at what was happening.

"Get down, right now or this will be over faster than you want it to be," the short one barked. "If you resist, you'll save me the trouble of arresting you, because you will be dead." Caleb knew he had to comply. They obviously were sent after him for a certain reason and would not hesitate to shoot if they thought he would fight. They had every right to kill him if he refused. Even if he didn't refuse, they could still kill him by law.

Caleb raised an arm. "Getting down." With his other hand, he patted Bandana's neck to calm her down and whispered, "It'll be alright, girl." Then, he swung his leg over Bandana and slowly slid to the ground, keeping his eyes fixed on the two Light-horsemen. The short one motioned to his partner, pointing to a rope that he carried. The big man dismounted, taking the rope. He walked slowly toward Caleb.

"On your knees, slave." He shoved Caleb, but was not strong enough to push him to the ground. The short one on the horse re-aimed his pistol at Caleb. Caleb backed up a few steps and kneeled.

The big Light-horse growled, "Hands behind your back, slave." The big man bound Caleb's wrists together with part of the rope and when the knot was secure, he wound more of the rope around Caleb's neck, holding onto the remainder like a life-threatening leash.

THE FREEDOM GAME

The crowd was getting loud. This was not just any slave being abused by Light-horse men with guns. They had seen that before. This was their beloved Caleb, the builder of their church, the church where they had come to worship. I could feel the righteous anger rising in the crowd. Reverend Watson truly cared about Caleb, but he knew he couldn't get too involved. From the door of the church he called out, "Please don't hurt him." The shout from the preacher startled both Light-horse men, who looked around defensively, suddenly aware that they were surrounded by two dozen slaves who apparently cared very deeply about what happened to their prisoner. The Light-horse men waved their guns around in the general direction of the crowd, but those guns were the old, single shot kind. Even if they each carried two weapons each, that was only four loaded shots for an angry crowd of twenty or more. Two Light-horse would be no match for this crowd once the four shots were fired. They knew it, and I could see fear lurking behind their threats.

The short one screeched, "Back off. All of you. We are here on official business." He spoke as clearly and authoritatively as he could, yet he was sweating and wiping his face repeatedly with his sleeve as he said, "This is a wanted slave. He is a criminal. And we have a written order for his arrest from the Council." He pulled out a soiled, rolled-up sheet of paper from his saddle bag. The crowd hushed, for the moment. He poked Caleb with the paper and laughed nervously. "Here. You can read it for yourself, if you want," he told Caleb. His laugh turned mocking, so sure was he that Caleb would be unable to read it. Slaves couldn't read. But there was a slave who could read it.

In a low voice, to myself, I said, "They don't call me Book Boy for nothing." Suddenly, I felt a surge of pride from that fact. Forgetting how scared I was a minute before, I called out from the church steps, high up enough over the crowd for everyone there to hear me, "I can read!" I jumped down and pushed my way through the crowd to the very center of the danger, still calling out, "I can read! I know how to read! I can read it to you, Caleb!" All eyes were on me now, including those of the two men holding pistols. The Light-horse stared at me with anger and disbelief. The metal of their gun barrels caught the sunlight and gleamed in my eyes, blinding me for a second. A cold fear washed over me when I realized what I had done by calling attention to myself. I had put myself in the most danger I'd ever been. This wasn't a small lie to Missus about a magazine. Those were bullets of death ready to be unleashed on me at their whim. But my fear wasn't only from the gunmen, either. Everyone was waiting for my next word. I had never spoken to so many people all at once before and what I would say would be the most important words I'd ever said before. My hands, usually steady, were trembling. I wondered, could everybody in Webb's Bend hear my heart pounding?

Caleb's voice brought me back to myself, and I forgot my fear as he said, "It's okay, son," in a hoarse whisper. "Just read it to me best you can. I could use a little help right now from a friend." He winked at me. His face looked so serene to me. I thought, how could a man be so close to what might be his own death and still have a face so kind and calm? I had always believed him to be a good man, but now his courage shone through like he was lit up with the brightest of lights. I knew everyone around us could see it, too, because they hushed. He looked around, nodding to them that everything would turn out fine. Even though I admired him more than ever in that moment, I was as sure as I could be that it would not turn out fine. I looked up at the tall Light-horse. He held the wrinkled paper taken out of the saddlebag in his fist. I had the feeling that he couldn't read it either and that he had been told why he was there to take Caleb. The paper was just to make it look more official. He would just pretend to know what was written. In fact, with the exception of Reverend Watson and maybe some of the rich folks there, I was just about the only one who could read it. This was my job and I would try my best to do it well.

The tall one sneered down on me. "What did you say, boy?" His lip curled up in an ugly mixture of hate, impatience at an African slave wasting his time, and wildness at the temptation to shoot me. I don't mind saying that I was scared.

"My name is Book Boy," I said, emphasizing the word Book.

The Light-horse man laughed a little. "That's a stupid name for a slave. Why would they call you that?"

"Like I said. I can read." I taunted him with his ignorance. "I can read that to you if you want to know what it says." I pointed to the paper.

He pointed the gun at me in anger. I was going too far. "You don't think I can read it for myself? I read it already, Book Boy. Let's just see if you really can read it." He thrust the paper toward me, then withdrew it, teasingly. "But if you can't," he chuckled, "if you can't... I'll shoot your eyes out of your slave head and you won't read nothing anymore! How about that, Book Boy?"

I slowly reached out my unsteady hand. I was sure I could read it, but what if he told me I read it wrong? He could shoot me dead right then and there. He could shoot a slave and not think twice about it, especially a slave whose best asset was that he could read. I was not worth as much money as slaves who could work with cattle, build, or fix things. I bet myself that he would kill me, whatever I read, but I was committed. I didn't want to stop. I could actually feel myself get a little stronger. There was something special about me now. I wasn't just looking on, like the other slaves. I had a purpose here, at this very moment. I was at the center. I felt a new kind of importance, being willing to place myself in danger to help Caleb. It felt good. This was far beyond any good feeling I got from helping Missus. It wasn't the pat-on-the-head because you did what you were told feeling. It wasn't even like tricking Roger Ficklin to help Misty. This was me, out in the open, not pretend. I realized where I had felt this before. It was a freedom game feeling come to life, like when I would imagine myself doing something because I wanted to do it, because I was free, not because I had to do it. I was scared, it's true. Who wouldn't be with those two waving their pistols around? But I also felt good, free good. It tasted so sweet I almost forgot to be afraid. That might have been the first time in my life I ever felt really free.

I reached out and grabbed that piece of paper. It smelled like his saddle-bag, leather and trash. I carefully spread it open, smoothing out the wrinkles the best I could. The Light-horsemen looked as interested in hearing what it said as much as Caleb and the other slaves did. Reverend Watson was listening, too, and the rich worshippers. Only a few people had run away, scattering in different directions when the guns came out. The chattering and jockeying stopped. Everybody got so quiet and still, focused on my every move. I looked over the paper in silence. It's not that I was trying to tease them, making them wait. I really just wanted to be sure I could read it before I opened my mouth. As I held the paper, I noticed that my hands had stopped trembling. Was I actually enjoying the attention, or did it feel like one of my freedom game adventures come to life? Whatever the reason, a clear, strong voice came out of me as I began to read.

"Alright everybody. Alright." I cleared my throat a few times even though I didn't really have to. "Here's what it says." I spoke slowly and carefully. "Being that the code of the Cherokee Nation prohibits..."

From the crowd, someone asked, "What does peribit mean?"

I answered, "I think it means you're not allowed to do it." I continued reading, "prohibits a slave from owning any kind of property," I paused for a second to look up, as though I needed a gulp of air, "and the slave known as Caleb owned by the Cherokee family Vanner has been claiming that he owns the horse he calls Bandana, that he feeds and grooms the horse and rides the horse every day, said slave Caleb has surely been found to be breaking the law." The crowd grumbled. People made angry sounds. I needed quiet again, so I raised my hand. "There's more. Quiet, please." When there was quiet, I continued reading. "The slave Caleb must therefore surrender the horse Bandana to the Light-Horse and also must suffer the punishment of 60 lashes on the bare back for his crime, punishment to be inflicted by the Light-horse." I looked up again to see that there were angry faces with shouts of 'No' coming from all over. Once more, I raised my hand for quiet. "Let me finish. If the slave should resist in any way, abusing any free person, he must suffer an additional sixty lashes on the bare back for each offense to be inflicted by the Light-horse."

As if in a single voice, the entire crowd of church people present let out a cry of disapproval, shaking their heads and waving their hands. I heard them say things like, "That's not fair! No! That's Caleb's horse! Imagine lashing him for caring for a horse! Terrible!" The grumbling got louder, angrier at the idea a slave could be treated so badly, so unfairly, even a slave like Caleb, who worked hard for his master and never complained. The angriest face, though, was Caleb himself. I had never seen him like that before. No longer calm, he looked somehow twisted up, half like he was about to cry, half like he wanted to kill someone. He grimaced at the Light-horsemen. The look was so horrible, they seemed afraid of him, shrinking back a little, even though they had the guns and he was on his knees.

Reverend Watson could see there was serious trouble coming from his congregation. There might even be violence involving his slave parishioners. He would be blamed for preaching freedom. If that happened, his church would be shuttered and he would be run out in disgrace. He tried to work his way through the crowd to position himself between the Light-horsemen and Caleb. In as soothing a voice as he could find and still be heard, he said,

THE FREEDOM GAME

"Can we talk about this, please?"

"Nothing to talk about," the short one replied in a gruff voice, all the while watching Caleb. "You heard my orders. We take the horse and then we lash the slave. Period. Just like it says." He swung his gun around, pointing toward every part of the circle of slaves that had been advancing closer and closer an inch at a time. "Anybody, I mean anybody," he looked straight at me, "gets in the way, he will be hurt. Bad. Real bad." The crowd continued moving in. At this distance, they might easily overrun the two Light-horse-men. "Get back. Get back, I said." They didn't get back. There was constant shouting from all those encircling us, Caleb, the Light-horsemen and me, all the slaves unable to contain how they felt about the injustice to Caleb. I had never seen slaves behave in this way, as if something hidden in shadows had suddenly, irresistibly broken loose from their souls. Whatever spirit it was had nearly taken over, almost replacing the fear of the master and the gun. There were threatening gestures and fists raised. There were reckless words of not taking it lying down. I could feel the heat of the crowd. I could feel the pain of a long-felt emotional wound that had suddenly opened wide.

Then a single voice began to sound above the noise. The voice spoke a simple phrase, "Let Caleb go." Another joined in. "Let Caleb go." Then another and another, in unison, "Let Caleb go." Soon every slave in the crowd was shouting the words, "Let Caleb go." It was a roar of defiance. Some held hands. Some locked arms. "Let Caleb go." There was a new sense of strength. A cloud of choking, dry dust rose from the road where we stood. It hung in the air, making it difficult to see clearly. The tall Light-horse pan-icked. With a piercing bang, his gun went off, cutting through the noise. The crowd fell silent, but the sharp sound set off Bandana. The frightened horse began bucking and kicking, first her hind legs, then raising up her fore legs. She made a pitiful, shrieking noise. Bandana's wild kicking was conta-gious. The other horses became agitated, too, kicking up their front legs and coming down hard. If you were underneath when those metal-clad hooves landed the weight of the horse on the hard earth, your bones would surely be broken. You could be killed. With his free hand, the tall Light-horse clutched his horse's mane with all his strength, trying desperately to grab the reins and pull him back. This caused his other arm to wave about wildly, which meant that his gun hand was out of control. In the confusion, we were all frightened, but more mad than anything. Sensing his weakness, some slaves

37

moved at him, threatening to rush him, though none had yet dared to touch him. Then, we heard another shot fired. It seemed to echo strangely in my ears. It was a sound that was bigger than an ordinary shot, marking the end of one thing and the beginning of another. The crack of the gun was followed by a crashing thud. Bandana had fallen to the dusty ground. I could make out a trickle of shiny, red blood as it streamed down the middle of her forehead. Her eyes were wide open, but had a dull, glazed look, as if nothing mattered to her anymore. She was still and silent. Everyone was stunned by the gunshot, frozen for a few seconds. Then they understood. The animal that nearly every slave there knew, many with affection, at the center of the commotion, the excuse for why this terrible wrong was being done, had been murdered by the careless bullet from a Light-horse gun. The crowd was enraged. Its last shred of caution turned to raw emotion, with some rushing right up to the Light-horse man, screaming threats in his face. The two who had come to take control had lost control and were now looking for a way out of danger. Despite their threats, the Light-horse men knew that slaves were valuable property and a massacre would bring the anger of wealthy slave owners down on their heads. All they wanted now was to find a way to take their prisoner and leave the angry mob far behind.

In the confusion, I saw an opportunity. Only a few feet away from where I stood, Caleb was holding Bandana's head, limp in his arms. I ran to him and grabbed his arm. He looked up a me with sorrowful, helpless eyes. "Caleb, you have got to get out of here," I said in a low, firm voice. Until that moment, I didn't even know I had that voice in me. "Now. Right now." He nodded and took a last look at his beloved horse. There was no question that Bandana was his horse, whatever the evil paper may have said differently. Even in death it was true, and Caleb was feeling the shock and sadness of having seen her killed. The anger and sorrow must have been overwhelming for him, but I couldn't let that stop him from saving himself. As soon as they were able, the Light-horsemen would try to take him. I grabbed Caleb's sleeve and led him, half-crouching. We circled around to the other side of the shouting people. Then we ran hard.

CHAPTER 4

The Light-horse men were too busy pushing the slaves away from their horses to notice us. By the time they were both mounted and ready, we had vanished. Without hesitation, I headed us in the direction of Jumping Ben and Miss Annie's cabin in the woods near the river. The first place, the only place, I thought of going was to Jumping Ben's shed. No one but Ben and I ever went there. No one else ever had reason to go there, so I wouldn't expect us to be found just by chance. As far as I knew, I was Ben's only visitor since Annie's family moved to Texas. The house and shed were surrounded by woods, with the river running in back of the shed. It was deep in the woods. You had to walk on a path about a half mile long to get there from the nearest road. Between the thick trees, the path was too narrow for a wagon, barely wide enough for a horse in some spots. It was November, so the path was lined with red and yellow leaves that had fallen from trees of the same colors. The trees came right up to the edge of the glassy river which reflected the perfect, cloudless blue sky. The days were cooling off and the nights were getting cold, but the shed would block the cold wind that blew off the river. It was as good a place to hide as any and we were in too big a hurry for me to come up with another spot. We just had to convince Jumping Ben and Miss Annie.

We had been running ran as fast as we could since Bandana was shot and were both getting tired. Caleb was breathing heavily, half talking to himself, "I just can't believe Bandana is dead. There was just no reason for this. We did no harm to anyone, ever. None at all." He suddenly turned to me and grabbing my arms, held me still. He looked me in the eye. His large, strong hands easily stopped my running. "Book Boy, if we go back now, I'll get a hundred lashes and you'll just go back to Missus. But, if you help me to run away, they'll hang us both, dead."

"That's only if they catch us." My words were brave, but I was trembling with fear, inside. He could probably hear the quivering in my voice.

"Book Boy, I can't do this to you," he said in low, serious voice, shaking his head.

"No! You're not doing anything to me. They are. I'm helping you. I don't care. Now, let go of me. Besides, I have an idea. A great idea."

"Now look here, boy. I mean it. You get out of here. You got me this far. Thank you. That's enough." Caleb shoved me to the ground. "Stay there. I'll be okay."

"You won't be okay." I felt tears streaming down on my face. "They will find you and they won't just lash you, they'll hang you and kill you whether I'm there or not."

Caleb looked at me in wide-eyed silence. He knew that I was right. Then he spoke softly, "There's nothing you or anyone can do. Somebody decided a slave had too much freedom and they needed to put an end to it, to teach the other slaves a lesson."

"No! There's a way, Caleb. I know a way. I truly do. You got to let me tell you."

His expression changed. "Alright, son." He laughed a little and rubbed my head. "You just won't give up, will you? Well, let's hear it. What's this great, magical thing you got in your head that's gonna save us?"

Seeing him smile made me smile. Then I started laughing right out loud. I didn't think I would ever be able to tell another soul my secret plan, but now I had to tell him. He needed my plan if he wanted to get out of this alive. I guess it was such a relief to finally get this out and hear it spoken, that I just wanted to laugh and shout.

Caleb started laughing. "Oh, it's that good, huh? You got a plan so good you laugh just thinking about it?" He got serious again. "We're running out of time. Let's have it. Now."

"I don't exactly have all the details reckoned yet, but here it is. First, you got to get out of sight. Somewhere we can get to quick, where you can stay for as long as it takes to get ready. A place they'll never find you."

Caleb agreed, nodding. "You have a place like that?"

"I think so. I have these friends. I read for them sometimes and I visit them a lot. They're Cherokees and ..."

Caleb's face dropped. "No. I'm not risking Cherokees. I don't care if you read them the whole Bible."

I insisted. "You don't understand. They don't like slavery. They live in the woods away from everybody. Jumping Ben goes into town only to work when he needs cash money. Otherwise he and his wife Miss Millie just hunt in the woods and fish in the river and raise a few vegetables."

"Oh, Jumping Ben? That's your friend? I worked with Jumping Ben a while back. He's a good hunter. I remember him going into the woods and coming back in ten minutes with something to cook."

"Right. That's him. And I bet you saw right away that he didn't treat you like you were a slave."

"I do remember, I liked him straight off. He seemed like an honest man. But what makes you think he'll risk everything for a runaway slave?"

I started losing my patience with Caleb's questions, knowing our head start on the Light-horse was running out. My voice was getting louder and faster. "I don't know. I'm not sure if he will. He might turn us in." I was shouting, now. "He might shoot us. I don't know, but he is our only hope right now. So let's just go there and let me talk to him. Please."

Caleb sighed and gave me the look an adult gives a kid who'd better be right. He waved his arm forward. "Show me the way, son."

Through the trees, I could see the horizon and I recognized that it was the ridge paralleling the road. I told Caleb, "On the other side of that ridge is the road. If we follow that road to the right, we'll come to the path that runs through the woods, leading to Ben's house. Follow me." From somewhere, maybe it was knowing that Caleb depended on me, I got a burst of energy. Minutes before, I was exhausted enough to just let myself land on a bed of leaves and stay there. Now, I had all the strength I needed and I climbed through the woods up to the ridge, sprinting like a deer. Caleb followed closely behind me. He waded through the leaves, tired, but determined. We made it to the ridge and looked down on the road. The road was empty, which was a comfort, yet we both understood that if anyone saw us, slave or free, it would get back to the Light-horse where we were. The whereabouts of a runaway slave, a fugitive from Light-horse punishment at that, was big news. They would tell someone else, who would tell some else and the chain would only end when it gave us away to the Light-horse men. You can be sure all of Webb's Bend, free and slave, was talking and guessing about it by now. Maybe we had been spotted already while running from poor Bandana's limp body.

I was worried indeed as we crept along, clinging to the rise on the side of the road to keep from being seen as best we could. The sharp blue sky and bright sunshine didn't help. It would be easy enough for anyone passing by to see us no matter how carefully we tried to keep from view. I was worried, too, about Jumping Ben's reaction. I knew he and Miss Annie liked me, but risking their lives for Caleb? There needed to be more. There was one thing about Ben that crossed my mind, making me think that there could be a reason for him to help us. Recently, I was in the town, doing or getting something for Missus and I saw Ben arguing with another Cherokee. I had never seen him angry before, so I was curious and moved close enough to overhear what they were saying. I could only make out that one of the other Cherokee's sons had killed one of Ben's relations, I think a sister's boy. This wasn't unusual. Some Cherokee families held grudges against each other for years and years. It was a problem for the slaves, too, because, being the property of one family made us targets for another family's revenge. Taking or killing someone's slave was a way to get even. It occurred to me that Caleb's situation might somehow be connected to a Cherokee feud.

We finally came to the turnoff through the woods that would take us to Ben and Annie's place. Without speaking, I pointed to the opening of the path. Caleb understood and slipped in between the trees behind me. When we were well into the woods, I asked him, "Caleb, who might want to hurt Mr. Money Joe by putting the Light-horse men onto you?"

"You think that's why they were there for me and Bandana? Somebody was mad at Money Joe?"

"I do. But who? You see anybody arguing with him lately?"

"You know, I did see something last week that stuck with me. There was this other Cherokee slave owner who stopped Money Joe in town. He was kicking up quite a fuss, yelling at Mister Money Joe, shaking his fist, swearing something awful. He was surely loud enough for everybody to stop cold whatever they were doing and look to see what was going on. The other Cherokee told Money Joe that he better control his family, the Vanners. That he keep them all away from his daughters and his slaves. I never saw Mister Joe look scared before, but he did then. Mad, too. After that, he told me to pass the word that slaves can't go anywhere alone. He said we could only go out if we were with someone else. Especially the girls and the young ones had to have someone with them. I reckon he saw trouble coming from that other Cherokee man.

"And the trouble must've come straight to you, Caleb," I said, sure that we had figured it right. Those Light-horse men were sent to get Caleb by Mr. Money Joe's enemy. Mr. Money Joe couldn't stop him either, because the law was dead against Caleb. The law said slaves were not allowed to own anything and that included Bandana. Mr. Money Joe's enemy knew just what he was doing. Now the trouble was on Caleb. Ben's clearing was within view. I asked Caleb, "I wonder if Jumping Ben is related to Mr. Money Joe?" Caleb saw where I was heading with this. We were close enough to the house that I thought it best to whisper. "If Jumping Ben is part of the Vanner family, he may want to help us just to spite the family's enemy. I'll feel him out slowly."

I heard a twig crack behind us. We swung around to find Ben pointing a musket at us. "Hello, Book Boy." He nodded his head at Caleb. "I think I know who you are. Yup. You're that slave the whole world is turning upside down trying to find, aren't you?" He motioned with the musket toward the house. "Get inside there. Go on, get in there, quick."

"Sure, Ben," I said. That was the second time in my life that anyone had ever pointed a gun at me, the first time being the Light-horse pistol that morning. I didn't like it much, but I was strangely getting used to it. I was still surprising myself.

Caleb planted himself in front of me, raising his hands slowly. "We're going. We're going. Just please don't point that at the boy, he's not a part of this trouble."

Ben looked more serious than angry. He motioned again with the musket. "Keep moving."

We walked up to the house, Ben following with his musket still on us. The door was opened by Miss Annie on the inside. She looked as though she expected us. "Come on in. I got some stew in the pot. You boys hungry? I'll bet my last good needle you are." Now she was smiling. She might even have been giggling a little. I was bewildered. Caleb and I didn't say a word.

We sat down on the two chairs Annie had put at the table which was already set with two bowls and two spoons. She lifted the heavy pot that hung in the rock fireplace and proceeded to scoop out stew portions into the bowls. Standing over us, she said, "Eat. Go on. I know you're hungry after running around crazy all morning." There was that giggle again. She certainly was pleased with the whole situation, but why? We looked at the food and tore into it like we hadn't eaten for a week. Maybe it was because I was so hungry, but that stew was the tastiest stuff I had ever had in my mouth. I felt better and better with every bite.

I came up for air. "Thank you, Miss Annie. This sure is a great stew. Thank you."

She stroked my head. "I'm glad you like it Book Boy. It's Ben's favorite."

I had forgotten about Ben. "I'm sorry, Mr. Ben," I said. "I hope we don't make any trouble for you. We had nowhere else to go and ..."

Annie interrupted me. "You're okay for now, boy. We know everything. Ben's been tracking you. We thought you'd be here a while ago."

Caleb lifted his head from the food, "Does anyone else know we are here, Miss?"

"No one but Ben and Wolfie." She pointed to an old dog who lay still near the fire.

"Ben," I said, "You know what happened this morning?" He nodded. "You think it was right, what they were going to do to Caleb?"

Ben put his musket, still loaded, back on the rack where it hung on the wall. "No, I don't. I don't think it's right for one man to own another man. But that's the law. I say we get ourselves rid of that law. But there's more to what happened than that. You boys got caught up in a big mess. Annie can tell you."

We all looked at Miss Annie and found her smiling. "Yes, I know what happened and I'm glad you got away." Then, her expression changed to anger. "I'm sorry for your horse, Caleb, but I'm thankful you got away. They didn't care so much about you. The Light horse men were only there to hurt my brother, Money Joe Vanner." I must have looked surprised. "I guess you never knew that, Book Boy." She laughed. "That's one reason why he never minded you coming to see us here by yourself. I should have said, he's my half brother. We had the same father, but not the same mother. I do love my brother, but the truth is, I don't like the way he lives. What I mean is, I don't like that he lives off slaves, gets rich off slaves. He knows I don't approve. When we were growing up, even though we saw each other a lot, we didn't ever live together. He was raised in a big house with a lot of slaves, like where he is now, and I always lived in a place like this, like you see me here. We used to talk about it. He tried to get me to come live with him and once or twice I almost did. Then I met Ben. But the Vanners aren't the only rich Cherokee family. I think you might know the William family. Mr. Robert William also got a big house with plenty of slaves to work his farm, so you'd think Money Joe and Mr. Robert would have a lot in common, and they do. For instance, they both want to keep their African slaves just as they are, doing the work and making them rich. But the Williams have been fighting the Vanners for as long as I can remember. When I was a little girl, we kids were told to always stay away from the Williams kids, that their parents would come and snatch us away and do terrible things to us. It was true that every few years there would be a fight that ended in somebody getting hurt or maybe killed. This here's the most recent fight between them. Money Joe says the land at Red Valley is Vanner land and that's what I always thought, too. Robert William says that it's William land and tried to get the Council to agree. The Council won't make a decision because they don't want to make Joe mad. Then, Money Joe sent you, Caleb, up to the valley to set up how they could clear it to start farming. That's how Robert William saw you on your horse."

Caleb stopped her. "Wait. That was Mr. Robert who asked me about my horse up in the valley?"

"Must have been." Annie continued, "You likely told him Bandana belonged to you. He finally found a way to slow down old Money Joe by getting at you. It's against the Cherokee law for a slave to own anything. If Joe is responsible for that law being broken, Robert William could use that to ruin him. The crazy thing is, now old Joe wants to get you, too. These stupid slave owners care more about controlling their slaves than anything. So, I'm glad you got away, even if old Joe is riled." Annie got very serious. "I'll tell you this. You may have made all the slave owners mad at Robert William for starting it all, but when they find you, I believe they aim to hang you and that's a true fact. Those slave owners can't let a slave who breaks the law and runs from the Light-horse get away with it."

I looked at Caleb. His eyes looked far away, like he was seeing his own death already. I could see it, too. He may have escaped the lash today, but the noose waited for him tomorrow. "Miss Annie, Mr. Jumping Ben, would you allow my friend Caleb here to stay in your shed until we can figure what to do?"

Ben was shaking his head even before I finished the words, saying, "I don't..."

I dropped to my knees. Choking back tears, I pleaded, "If someone comes looking, Caleb will just run off like he was only running right through your place to the river, and no one will ever, ever know he stayed here even one minute at all. Please, Mr. Ben. I'll read for you and Miss Annie any time, day or night."

Ben and Annie looked into each other's eyes. "This could get rough," Ben spoke softly to Annie. "We get caught, old Robert William would want us hung, maybe Joe would want that too, for stealing his property."

Annie was quiet. She knew it would be Ben to bear the worst of it should something go wrong. She put her hand on her mouth, then said, "Jumping Ben should do what is in his heart to do." She loved Ben and they had lived together for a long time. They had seen their share of danger, but never put themselves in the thick of it on purpose. Helping an escaped slave was new territory for them. Doing it would cross sacred lines of law and family. It was the most important decision they ever had to make. Now it was on Ben to decide.

Ben turned to Caleb. "How long?"

Caleb's face lit up. It sounded like Ben might say yes. "I don't really know. I got to get a plan of what to do next and I don't know how long that will take. I can tell you that I have no wish to stay around Webb's Bend any longer than necessary. Mr. Ben, Miss Annie, I know what this means and if you do this, you will always be in my prayers."

"Well, I'm not a Bible man," Ben said, "yet I do appreciate the notion. Okay, we'll find a place for you, but only until you make your plan to leave for good and all."

I jumped to my feet, shouting, "Yee Haw! Yee Haw!" Caleb was grinning. Miss Annie smiled and Jumping Ben looked worried. Caleb wisely held me down from dancing and put his hand over my mouth to keep me from making noise. Suddenly I realized how late it was. The sun was going down and I would be missed for supper if I didn't get going home. I stepped right in front of Ben and Annie. "Thank you," I said in my most sincere and polite voice. I meant it. Miss Annie hugged me. "I have to go now, before they start looking for me at the plantation." I turned to Caleb. "I'll be back."

Caleb took my shoulders in his big hands and quietly spoke, "Book Boy, you're the best, finest friend anyone could want. Thank you for being my friend." I looked away, though I'm not sure why. I guess I was embarrassed at being made a fuss over. I wasn't used to being appreciated like that, by a man I admired. I waved my hand and said goodbye. As I left the modest cabin, it came to me that I was entering a whole new part of my life. I walked back through the woods and thought. I had helped a fellow slave to escape, I had deep secrets from Missus and Mr. Money Joe and I had experienced events that, till then, I had only dreamed up before, playing the freedom game. For me, there was no going back to being all slave. I was part free and I liked the feeling, even though I was scared, very, very scared. I made up my mind that I would never be all slave again. I would do everything I could to be all free, all the time and not just in my head. That's when the questions started to bounce back and forth inside me. First, I scolded myself for being such a silly, helpless slave boy, who didn't know anything about the world, thinking I could be free. Where did I come off even wanting such a thing that could never be? I could see Missus waving a switch in my face, with a downright mean look in her eyes. She would tell me I was born a slave and that's all I was. Did that mean I'd have to stay a slave forever? I thought, how could a slave boy like me, needing my mistress and master for food, clothing, a place to sleep, everything, possibly live as anything but a slave? Just look at Caleb. He was a full grown man, strong and respected. People depended on him. He knew so much about the world. He knew how to fix things, how to make things, how to handle any job. Even Caleb wasn't free after all his years as a slave. What chance did I have? Still, he wasn't the same Caleb as yesterday, was he? He was hiding, he was scared, true enough. Was he as much a slave as he was yesterday? Yesterday, he jumped to do whatever Mr. Money Joe told him to do. Today, it doesn't matter what Mr. Money Joe wants him to do. Caleb is thinking for himself. And the reason he had to think for himself is because, today, he is nobody's slave. He would have to go far away to live his new, free life. Me, too, maybe. I could do it. Not on my own at first, but if

I escaped with Caleb, I'd surely be free!
　　Then I knew, I couldn't let this pass me by.

CHAPTER 5

As I came to my decision, I reached the road. I started running toward home, wanting to avoid any questions about why I was so late for Sunday supper. That was not to be. The minute somebody saw me set foot on the east side of the Vanner plantation, where I ate and slept, the shouting from slave to slave began, each one calling out to the other that I had come home. "Book Boy is back, Book Boy is back." A couple of east side children took me by the arms and lead me to the front of the slave house where Tall Bone slept. Many of the slaves had already started their meal there. Tall Bone stood up from the big wooden table where we took most of our meals in good weather. There was a hush of quiet. Everyone put their eyes on me. It was clear they thought I was the bringer of important news. Usually, I was more or less ignored during our meals. Not tonight, though. Tall Bone motioned for me to sit next to him. That was the first time he ever wanted me there. Any other night, I would have been lucky to get a seat at all. I didn't mind not eating at the table. Nearby, there was a nice maple tree with a thick trunk and twisted roots that swelled up out of the earth. I always thought of it as my spot. I had a real fondness for that tree. I could use those roots as a table and chair. Sometimes I would come to that spot just to lie on my back and watch the leaves move in the wind, letting the sunlight sparkle through from above. Being late fall, the daytime sky was very, very blue and the air so clear it felt like you could see for endless miles. Today's supper was different. My tree would have to wait because there was business to do. I walked over to Tall Bone. He had a rib in his hand and used it to show me where to sit. As his name implied, he was a tall man, with a long stride, though not as muscular as Caleb. He also was not as easy to talk to as Caleb. Most of what Tall Bone had to say was only what he needed to say. No jokes, no pleasantries, all business. If you worked with him, you better not make a mistake. I once saw him beat another slave for cutting wood the wrong length. Tall Bone hit him with his fist so hard that the man was lifted right off the ground and fell back down, out cold. It wasn't that he was looking out for Mr. Money Joe's interest, mind you. Everybody knew that Tall Bone hated Mr. Money Joe. He hated being a slave. He hated that he sweated to make another man rich. No, he was mad about the wood because it would take more time to finish the day's work. He only did precisely what he was told to do and no more. I heard him say, "How can a slave be proud of the work he does for the master and still have his own pride in himself?" People said Tall Bone had many children and not only with our plantation women. He would sneak off some nights to meet slave women from other farms. Once, when we used to sleep in the same slave house, I heard him come in real late. I sat up and looked at him. He smiled and put his finger over his mouth. That was the only time he ever smiled at me. I guess he was having a good night.

As I sat on the wooden stool, the people around the table looked at me as if they had already made their best guesses about Caleb and me, and now needed confirmation. Rose was there, taking care of me, as always. She dipped her hand into a pot on the table and came up with a couple of ribs which she put on metal plate. She added a few spoons of greens, gathered from a garden she grew herself. Missus thought it was her garden, but it was Rose who planted, tended and harvested the produce of that plot. Missus let Rose keep some if the crop was good. In bad years, Rose kept some anyway. She wasn't about to let any of us from the east side of the plantation go hungry. Her heart was full of love for all of us, like we were her children. Even the grown men, including Caleb and Tall Bone, respected Rose and put much stock in what she said. She didn't talk without thinking first, so when she did have something to say, it made good sense. You couldn't ignore it without being foolish. I loved her. I wished she was my mother, but I don't think she was. She probably was old enough to be my mother. In my early years, I thought she was the prettiest slave on the whole plantation, or anywhere else, slave or free. She put the plate in front of me and kissed me on the forehead. I instantly felt calmer, like everything was going to be alright. The day had been one frantic problem after another. I had more than enough excitement and just wanted to eat and then sleep. Rose could tell I was going through something big. She had an especially kind smile for me and putting her hand on Tall Bone's shoulder told him to, "Be gentle with the boy. He's had a hard day of it."

THE FREEDOM GAME

Rose once told me how she came to be a slave at the Vanner place. She was a young girl on a small farm where she and her mother were the only slaves. The white man who owned the farm had three children. His wife had died some years ago and Rose's mother took care of all the woman's work on the farm. She cooked, cleaned, sewed, tended the animals, whatever needed doing. Rose helped her mother in every way. One night, the man came home drunk with liquor. He was yelling and cursing. He carried on so loud it woke everybody out of their beds. Then he grabbed Rose's mother by the waist and pulled her toward him. He started touching her all over. She fought and screamed, wildly punching and clawing at his face, but he was a strong man and wouldn't let go. He threw her to the ground in front of all the children, including Rose, who was crying, not knowing what to do. In the fight, the few pieces of furniture there were in the house had been overturned and shoved around the room. Rose saw her mother fall next to the table. She saw a heavy iron pan on the table and grabbed it with both hands. Swinging wildly, with all her might, Rose hit the man on the head as hard as she could. He went limp for a minute and her mother pushed him off. The man started to come to his senses, holding his bleeding head. Her mother screamed for Rose to run away. At first, Rose wouldn't leave, but her mother was crying and begging her to run away, all the while trying to keep the man down. Rose dropped the pan and ran as fast and as far as she could. She kept to the road, but it was so dark, she could hardly tell where she was after a while. With no strength to go any further, she fell into a deep sleep, curled up by the side of the road. The next morning, she was awakened by the rumble of wagon wheels on the road. It was a supply wagon that had come from the trading post in Fort Gibson. It was making a delivery to Mr. Money Joe's place. The two men on board asked her how she ended up on the side of the road. Rose was too frightened to say anything. She just kept quiet. They decided not to leave her there on the road, so they picked her up, put her in the back of the wagon and brought her along. She made no attempt to resist them, worried about her mother, but glad to be leaving without having to run on her sore feet.

Late in the afternoon, after a long day's ride on a bumpy road, they arrived at the Vanner place. The men began to unload the goods from the back of the wagon. Missus always inspected the deliveries and made a careful accounting of every item she had ordered. When she looked into the wagon to see if the men had unloaded the full delivery, she noticed the frightened young African girl hunched down in the back of the wagon. Missus called to her, "Girl. Hey, Girl. What are you doing back there, girl?" Again, Rose said nothing. She was too scared, thinking about her mother and all that had happened to answer. She couldn't stop seeing the farmer's bleeding head in her mind. She had never even hit anyone before, let alone cause someone to fall and bleed. She wondered where the strength came from to do that.

Missus asked the men, "Please explain to me what you boys are doing with a young African girl in your wagon. I suspect that you two are up to something bad." Missus gave them a cold, hard stare.

They were afraid of Missus, but one, the wagon driver, was brave enough to talk. He replied, taking off his hat out of respect, "Missus, we only found the girl this very morning, just as you see her, sleeping on the side of the road. We couldn't just leave her there, now could we, Missus? We tried to talk to her, but she plain won't." The other one added, "I think there's something wrong with her. You know. Up here." He poked his partner's head.

Missus mulled it over. "Hmm. Alright boys. Tell you what. I'll give you five dollars for her. Now you listen. We don't know a thing about where this girl comes from or how she came to be lying in that road, so not a word about this to anyone. Understand? If you can't keep your mouth shut where you got the five, then no deal." Missus was sure the girl was a runaway slave, since just about every African girl in this part of the world was a slave. She didn't want the rightful owner to find out that she had gotten his property, and for the bargain price of five dollars.

"Ten?" the wagon driver said. Then he saw the bad look on Missus's face. That look scared most people. The driver held up his hands. "Whoa. Heh, heh," he laughed nervously. "Deal! The girl's all yours."

Missus called to young Rose, "Come on out here, girl. You're mine now. You belong to me. Mind what I say, and you'll be fine. Bad girls get the lash." Rose climbed down from the wagon. "Now go into the house and you'll find a table on the left with a center drawer. Take the five dollar bill out and bring it here. Do you know what a five looks like?" Rose shook her head, no. "Alright, then. Come with me and I'll show you. Go on. Quick as a bunny, now." Rose ran into the house, found the table, found the drawer, got the five and showed it to Missus. Missus grinned at the girl and stroked her head. They went back outside. "There's not a thing wrong with this pretty little head. She's pretty like a Rose. Rose, go back inside and we'll get you something to eat. Here's your five, boys. Best remember what I said." Missus handed them the five dollar bill. Rose had lived on the Vanner plantation ever since. She never knew what became of her mother after that.

Tall Bone had a real soft spot for Rose, and not only because she was beautiful. He trusted her completely. He knew she was smart and under-stood things in a way he couldn't. She was just about the only person who could talk sense into him sometimes. Tall Bone had a temper and people walked lightly around him. They knew he could go off on them if he thought they were against him in some way, like the slave who cut the wood wrong. If Rose was around, Tall Bone would look to her first and hesitate to use the violence that was his usual reaction. Nine times out of ten, Rose would calm him down and explain away what Tall Bone had taken for a harm. Then again, if Rose gave him the go-ahead to defend himself or punish an offender, it got pretty bad. Tall Bone could do a lot of damage before Rose put the brakes on him. That was another reason why people treated Rose with extra respect. Everybody knew that Tall Bone would take her side and not just with words. One time Rose left the cabin door open where about ten of us slept on the floor. Just before morning, the chickens found there way into the cabin and started pecking at us while we were asleep. It was kind of funny and most of us just laughed and shooed away the birds. Rose admitted that she had left the door open by mistake and told us that she was sorry. That wasn't good enough for Will, the stable slave. He was cussing and shouting something awful. He got up and walked over to Rose, who was still lying on the floor. Now, the chickens were scared, squawking and jumping. In the middle of the noise and wings flapping, Will raised his hand like he was going to hit Rose. Without warning, Tall Bone grabbed Will's fist as is was coming down, aimed at Rose's face. His big hand coved Will's entire fist and jerked it back with such power that we all heard the crack of Will's wrist bone breaking as it brought Will crashing to the ground. Tall Bone lifted his foot over Will's frightened face, ready to deliver a killing blow when Rose shouted, "Tall Bone, stop! That's enough. Thank you, Bone, I think he'll leave me alone, now." Tall Bone obeyed Rose's command, lay back down on his sleeping spot and started snoring.

That's why, after my long day, I could eat calmly, knowing that, even though I would soon be questioned by Tall Bone, Rose was there and I needn't be afraid. At the other end of the supper table sat Cotton Hand. He ate with his head down, looking at his plate of food. He didn't look up at me once. Still, he listened carefully to every word. It was his way not to look directly at anyone. Cotton Hand had been a slave all his life, mostly back east on a cotton plantation. Sometimes his owner would hire him out to other plantations, but always to pick cotton. He picked so much cotton, from morning to night, that the dried bristles on the plants would cut his hands, his wrists and his forearms all day, every day during the season, leaving him bloody. Cotton Hand had the scars to prove it. You couldn't help but notice the purple-red raised lines, bumps and patches when you looked at him. Every new person he would meet asked him how he got all those scars. He would lift up the hands they were so curious about and say, "Cotton Hand." The name stuck. He had only been on the Vanner place for three or four years. His master in the east, Georgia, I think, was a Cherokee, forced to move to the Indian Territory by the United States Government along with many other eastern Cherokees. They had to travel on foot, heading out in winter and, ultimately, walking a thousand miles before they were done. The going was so bad, they called it the Trail of Tears. Some of them brought their slaves with them, and Cotton Hand was one of those. Many of the Cherokees and their slaves died during the harsh trip. Cotton Hand managed to survive, but his original Cherokee owner died before reaching the Indian Territory. When Cotton Hand finally made it through the ordeal and crossed the Cherokee Nation boundary, he was auctioned off with other slaves whose owners had either died or simply needed the money. That's when Mr. Money Joe bought him at a cheap price to live and work on the Vanner plantation. Though conditions on the Vanner place were far better than the plantation he had known in the east, Cotton Hand had suffered so much during his life as a slave that he often mumbled about running away, nearly every day. Sometimes he would say it under his breath, sometimes for others to hear. He never actually tried, though because he was too afraid of getting caught. This was understandable. Where he came from, they wouldn't just lash a runaway, they would lash him and then hang him or shoot him, too, as an example to put fear into the other slaves, to prevent them from running. Instilling such fear worked on Cotton Hand when, the first time he, as a boy, saw what was done to a runaway slave who had been caught. Cotton Hand told the story that the master's dogs found the slave and dragged him out of the bushes with their teeth. Right there, the overseer called the slaves nearby to look and took the lash to the runaway's bare back. The lash hit the slave with such force that blood spattered everyone near him, including Cotton Hand. The slave was limp after about a hundred lashes, but they tied a noose around his neck anyway and hoisted him up on a tree branch. He hung there for days, to be seen by every slave on the plantation.

As Cotton told the story his face became more and more angry. To him, the very public murder of the slave didn't just instill fear of escaping, it also instilled hate. Cotton said, after that, he might do as he was told, but it wouldn't stop him from thinking up of all kinds of ways he wanted to kill the master and the overseers. I think, to preserve himself, he knew he had to obey, so, Cotton Hand found that he could transform his need to defy the master into imaginary plans for the master's death. He talked about it a lot. Sometimes, he would imagine that he was the one to kill the master. Other times it would happen as a lucky accident causing the master's demise. A rock, perhaps, thrown up carelessly by a wagon wheel, might strike the master at just the right spot on the head. Or he could picture a whipsaw, flying out of control to reach the master's throat. His hate knew no bounds in what his mind could cook up. Although he didn't physically murder his master on the Trail of Tears, he was sure that the death was the result of his long-time wish being granted. Cotton Hand carried that feeling of hate with him to the Indian Territory. Now it was Mr. Money Joe and Missus that he dreamed of killing. In private, he swore he would do it someday. On the Vanner plantation, everything around him became fuel for his murderous plans. If he had an axe in his hand, he thought of chopping Mr. Money Joe into small pieces. If he was holding a hammer, he thought of hammering Missus's head. It seemed to make him feel better to think about doing those things. He never attempted to follow through on any of the plans. The hate hardened him. Cotton Hand never smiled or seemed to enjoy anything, but he was never mean to me or to the other slaves as far as I could see. When out of the overseer's earshot, he would talk freely to us in a low, monotone about who he wanted to kill and how. I felt sorry for him, so consumed by hate. I hated being a slave, but I don't think I ever wanted to kill Missus or Mr. Money Joe. I just wanted to be free.

Sitting at the table, I was so tired I didn't think I had the strength to eat.

As I ate, the hunger took me over and I swallowed everything Rose put in front of me. Tall Bone could wait no longer. He leaned into me, insistently. His deep, rich voice demanded, "Book Boy, talk to us. We need to know what happened to Caleb. We only want to help him."

I had to protect Caleb's secret. "Mr. Tall Bone, I, I," I was stuttering. I had never stuttered before that. "Caleb, Caleb..."

Rose walked over to me. She shooed away the person sitting next to me and sat down, cradling me with her arm around my shoulder. "You can trust us, Book Boy. There's not a person at this table who doesn't want the best for our Caleb. Anything you have to say will stay right here with us and go no further. I promise."

I was sure that she meant her promise from the heart. It wasn't enough for me though, because she couldn't possibly speak for everyone there. I hardly knew some of the slaves that were wandering by after eating their supper. I wanted to tell Rose everything that happened. Tall Bone and Cotton Hand were Caleb's good friends, so they could know. I just didn't trust anyone else at the moment. Slaves would sometimes give information to the master in exchange for favors. Even a loose word overheard by the wrong person could be disastrous. I whispered in Rose's ear, "Only you, Tall Bone and Cotton Hand. I can't risk telling anyone else right now. That alright?"

She raised her eyebrows to Tall Bone and then to Cotton Hand. She whispered, "That's alright, dear." Then she whispered something to Tall Bone.

"Cotton, stay here," Tall Bone said sternly. "Everybody else, go." Somebody grumbled that they were still eating. Tall Bone stood up. "Take it with you and go. Leave. Now!" The table emptied quickly. Tall Bone sat back down and Cotton Hand joined us at the end of the table.

I felt better that I could speak softly without being overheard. "When the Light-horse shot Bandana and everyone at the church started kicking up a fuss, I pulled Caleb away from the crowd. He was so upset at seeing Bandana that way, he didn't even think about saving himself. That Light-horse man was getting ready to kill Caleb. I could see it in his face. When the dust got into everybody's eyes, that was our chance. The Light-horse was too blind and busy with the crowd to see us run. We took off. We ran through the woods and followed the ridge down to the road as fast as we could get through it.

"Why would you go there? People could have seen you on the road," Tall Bone wanted to know.

I answered, "The only good place I could think of to hide would be inside, somewhere. In the woods or down by the river, they could track us easily and with the leaves already starting to fall, they might even see us through the trees. They would find us in a day, at most. But, if we were indoors, they could only find us if they came to just the right house. That would be much harder to do, especially if it were the house of a Cherokee."

They looked at each other, first admiring my logic, then bewildered that I knew such a person. Cotton couldn't believe it. "You know a Cherokee?" he asked. "Wait. You know a Cherokee that would hide you? Come on, Book Boy, you telling us fibs? What Cherokee that you know has a house and would use it to hide you and Caleb? That doesn't sound like the truth to me, boy."

Rose defended me. "Book Boy would not lie. I never heard him lie. Ever. Go ahead, dear. Tell us what you and Caleb did."

I continued, "If you follow the ridge that runs next to the road for a while, then you have to get onto the road for a short distance. You come to a path through the woods that leads to a clearing and a house."

"What house is that?" Tall Bone asked. I hesitated. "Who lives in that house, Book Boy?"

"A Cherokee man and his wife live there," I said.

Rose gently put her hand on my head. "We can't help if we don't know."

"Alright," I said reluctantly. "It's the house of Jumping Ben and his wife, Miss Annie."

Tall Bone recognized the name. "I think I have heard of him. How do you know him?"

"They sometimes invite me to visit. Usually, it's when they want me to read something to them. A newspaper, a magazine, a letter. They can't read it themselves, so I help them out when I can. I've been reading for them for a few years, now. We are friends."

Cotton Hand grumbled. "Friends? With a Cherokee? And a slave? Never happen."

"Cotton Hand, they are my friends, truly. They are good woods people.

R. A. BLUMENTHAL

They don't own slaves. They don't like slavery. They think slavery is bad, bad for everyone, including Cherokees. I heard Jumping Ben say so. I heard it with my own ears."

"After you came to the house of these Cherokees, what happened?" Tall Bone asked.

"They told us that one of Mr. Money Joe's Cherokee enemies was trying to get even with him and that's why they sent the Light-horse after Caleb. Hurting Caleb would hurt Mr. Money Joe. Bandana was the excuse."

"Oh," Rose said. "That makes sense, yes. But, where is Caleb now?"

"I begged Miss Annie and Jumping Ben to let Caleb stay in their shed. It's tucked away, in back of the house, by the river. I promised to read for them any time they wanted. I always did that anyway, but I couldn't think of anything else I had to give them. I begged and begged. Then Miss Annie told me that she was related to Mr. Money Joe and didn't like what they did to Caleb. They agreed to let him stay for a few days until he made a plan for what he would do next. As far as I know, he's in their shed now. Please, please, please don't say anything to anyone about this. Please."

Tall Bone's usual tough look softened. I think he smiled, but I'm not sure. "Don't worry, boy. Caleb's secret is safe with us. No need to worry about that." He rubbed my head. "You did a great job, Book Boy."

Rose was proud of me. She hugged me and kissed my cheek. Even Cotton said I had done a good thing. All the praise felt good, but I knew I had to sleep. Rose could tell. She said, "Dear, dear boy, you go to bed now and sleep well. Let's all wake up an hour early tomorrow so we can talk more about this." I went straight to my place on the floor of the slave house and fell into a deep sleep. I know I slept for hours, but it seemed like just a few minutes later Rose was gently rousing me. "Book Boy," she said in a hushed voice, trying not to wake anyone else. "Book Boy. Come, dear. It's time." I stood up, still groggy, and walked outside into the fading night. The sun was not yet visibly rising, but the morning light that preceded it was already seeping into the black sky. I rubbed my eyes and made an effort to become fully awake. It was difficult after yesterday's ordeal. I needed more rest. Since this was the only time for us to be together before our morning work would begin, I had no choice. We met in back of the slave house where we had just been sleeping, but were aware that others could hear us if we were too loud.

58

We moved a few yards away from the house and spoke in whispers.

Tall Bone spoke first. "Here's the way I see it. Caleb can never come back. As valuable as he is, he's not just a runaway slave who can be lashed and forgiven. Damage was done, a horse was killed. The Light-horse will blame it on Caleb. They'll also say that Caleb refused his punishment for claiming to own the horse. All of this makes it almost certain that Caleb will be hung if they catch him."

"Then we have to help him get away," Rose said.

Cotton Hand shook his head, looking at Rose as if she were crazy, "Us help? How can we help, woman? What could we do?" he said in his usual monotone.

"Hush, Cotton. If you're going to talk, whisper," said Rose. "And try to say something good."

"We need to talk to Caleb and come up with a plan," I said. "I might have something." I knew exactly what I wanted to happen, but it wasn't the right time or place to tell them.

"Let's get to work now before somebody notices us. Meet here again tonight after everyone has gone to bed. Then we'll all go to Jumping Ben's place and talk to Caleb," Tall Bone said.

"Good," said Rose.

"I'll be here," said Cotton Hand.

"Me too," I said. As I turned to leave, I was startled to see the same two Light-horse men who killed Bandana slowly walking toward us.

"What are you slaves doing back here?" the short one said, eyeing us suspiciously.

"That's where we sleep, sir," said Rose. "We were saying our morning prayers before work, sir. We finished just now. Amen." We all repeated, "Amen."

"Prayers? Him?" the Light-horse pointed to Cotton Hand. "Ha! You do that every morning, or just when I'm here?"

Rose shot him a cold look. "Most mornings, sir."

He looked at me. "I know you. You're that freak slave who can read. I want to talk to you, boy."

"I'm late, sir. I got to get to work. Missus will be looking for me," I said.

"I'm looking for you, boy. And now I found you."

"I really got to go," I said, starting to leave. The big one grabbed me by the shirt and pulled me back, hard. I tripped and fell on the ground. He stood over me as I lay on the ground.

"I said I want to talk to you." He put his foot on my chest. The weight made it difficult for me to breathe. "You look mighty jumpy, boy. Something wrong? Don't you want to talk to me? You couldn't wait to talk yesterday, could you? Where's your friend? He left before we could finish with him and I want him back. Where did he go?"

"What friend?" I said, weakly.

"Oh. You want to do it like that? Sure. I don't mind. This might be fun." He bent down to put his face a few inches from mine. "How about this? I'll ask you one more time where Caleb is. You tell me and you can go to work. But you don't tell me, and my big partner, here, gives you a nice hard whack on your back with the whip. He's really good at whipping, too. He likes it. You ever been lashed, boy?" I made no answer. I was very scared. "No? Well, that's it, then. That's the trouble. Maybe somebody should have taken the lash to you a long time ago, to show you what's what. I say, every slave ought to be lashed regular, to keep their heads straight. Otherwise they get confused in their thinking. Let's try this again. Where is Caleb?"

"I don't know." My voice was trembling. It was true, I had never been lashed and didn't ever want to be. I wasn't going to tell him anything, though.

He lifted his foot and looked at his partner. "Go ahead," he said, grinning. The big man turned me over, face down in the dirt. He put his boot on my leg and pushed my shirt up to expose my bare back. Probably a minute went by. The anticipation of what was to come made it seem much longer. I couldn't see what was happening because I was face down. I felt sick to my stomach. Then I heard the crack of the whip. A stinging pain seared my back. I had never felt such a sharp pain before. I was sure he had split my skin. Was I bleeding? Then it began to throb as a welt swelled up on my skin.

Rose screamed, "No, don't hurt the boy! Please, don't hurt him." The lash came down on me a second time. It struck me in almost the same place and there was no doubt now that blood was flowing from my back. I had never felt pain like that before. It made me short of breath. I felt dizzy. There was bright sunshine, but the world around me started going dim. Another blow like that one and I might pass out. I needed to keep myself awake. I couldn't let the secret out, no matter how many times the lash came down. I couldn't risk what I might say if I were only half awake. In that condition, I could be tricked into talking. Rose's scream must have attracted attention because I could hear people talking all around me.

"Let's try again," the Light-horse said. "I ask you where Caleb is. You tell me and you get to go to work. You don't tell me and you get the lash. Understand? Good."

"No! Wait," I yelled.

"Ready to tell me?" the Light horse sneered. "It's okay, boy. Everybody breaks sooner or later."

I needed time to get my strength back before the next blow. "Uh...why are you asking me? How come you think I know where Caleb is? You can ask anybody. There's no one who's seen him since you killed his horse."

"I didn't kill his horse," the Light-horse said defensively.

"What! Everybody saw you kill his horse," I said. The slaves who had gathered to watch my lashing made it known that they agreed without actually speaking, afraid of being lashed themselves. Instead, they nodded and said, "Mhmm."

All except Rose, that is, who bravely said, "We all saw you, Mister. Everybody saw you kill Caleb's horse. You shot him right in the head and he fell over dead, poor thing."

He turned to Rose. "I couldn't have killed 'his' horse because a slave can't have a horse." He looked back at me. "And I'm asking you because you were the last person I saw with him."

"Then whose horse did you kill?" I said, desperately trying to delay the next blow I knew would come.

"I don't know and it doesn't matter," he said impatiently.

Another, familiar voice thankfully entered the conversation. "Mine." It was Missus's voice and she was angry. "The horse you killed was mine. You lost my slave and you killed my horse all in one, quick Sunday morning. And now what do you think you're doing with another of my slaves on the ground! Keep whacking him with that whip and he won't be any use to me either. Get up, Book Boy." I stood up, painfully. She shouted her orders to the Light-horse men. "Now you two get going and find the slave you lost. He's not here. If he were here, I wouldn't need you to go get him, would I?"

"Yes, Missus," they both said at the same time.

The slaves who had been holding their horses gladly handed them the reins. We watched them ride off and Missus shooed the slaves back to work. She walked over to me and looked at my back, shaking her head. "Why do you reckon they think you know where Caleb is hiding, Book Boy?"

"I don't know, Missus." I let out a cry of pain.

"Do you know where he is?" she asked.

"No, Missus. I don't know where he is now. I saw him run when they shot Bandana."

"I hope you aren't lying to me, Book Boy. Go to the big house. I'll send Misty to tend to your back."

"Yes, Missus." I ran to the big house. She didn't have to send for Misty, though. Misty was already there, at the front door, waiting for me. She looked like she had been crying.

"Come here, Book. My poor Book." As I walked in, she saw my back and gasped. "Lord in Heaven, what did those evil men do to you?" She led me to a water bucket in the kitchen. She took a rag and dipped it in the water, soaking the rag. Then she squeezed it onto my back. I winced, but it felt good and cool on the hot wound. She did that repeatedly, cleaning off the blood and dirt. "You're a brave one, my Book. Yes, you are. I heard they asked you for Caleb and you refused. You refused, even though they lashed you. My poor Book."

"It was Missus that saved me."

"Maybe she did stop them, but I think you would have taken more lashes instead of giving them Caleb. You would never have told them where he is. Even if they..."

I turned around so fast and grabbed her wrists so tightly, Misty was frightened. My eyes darted from side to side to see if anyone could hear us. "Misty, listen to me." I spoke each word slowly. "I don't know where Caleb is. So I could not tell them anything, anyway, anyhow. I don't know. Okay? Understand?" I realized that I may be hurting her and let go. "I'm sorry." I kissed her hand.

"It's alright, Book. I understand. I do." She went back to nursing my back. She saw how serious this had become for everyone. She leaned into me and spoke softly in my ear. "Whatever is going on, Book, please, I'm in. I'm with you."

I looked into her beautiful, dark eyes and for the first time that day, in spite of the pain from the wound, I felt happy. I was with her. She stroked my face with her graceful hand. Missus broke the moment, walking into the room loudly, her shoe heels striking the wood floor of the kitchen. I looked in her direction.

"Misty, leave us," Missus said. Misty instantly obeyed, putting the rag in the bucket and carrying the bucket out of the room. "Book Boy, come to the table and sit down." I did what she asked and she sat down across from me. "I want you to know how important this is for me and my family. Another Cherokee family is trying to hurt us, maybe even bring us down. Our two families have been fighting for generations. In the old days they would fight us with violence. Now, they are doing whatever they can to get our farm, our slaves and everything else we own and, instead of arrows, they are using the law to do it. They are the ones who sent the Light-horse to punish Caleb and take his horse. Yes, I said his horse. Who didn't know that Bandana was Caleb's horse? But me allowing him to have Bandana was also against the law. I could be punished, too. That's why it's so important that Caleb come back and tell how we never gave the horse to him, that we always told him he could use Bandana but he did not own Bandana. We have powerful friends on the Council, too, and even the words of a slave will help our case, to show we are being unfairly attacked. We need Caleb to come back. Tell me where he is."

"Missus, I don't know where he is. But if you did get him back, what would they do to him?" I asked.

"Boy, I will say this plainly. Caleb is a lost cause. No one can save him. If he runs, they hang him for running. If he comes back on his own, they will hang him for resisting arrest. He's as good as gone already and there's not a thing that you or me or anyone can do about it. You have to believe me, Book Boy. Caleb is dead. The only good he can do now is to help us fight off the ones who want to take our farm away, to take you away from me. If they win, you and all the other slaves will belong to someone else. They will not treat you good as me. They will beat you and they will whip you. The will give you scraps to eat and hard, hard labor to do in the burning sun. They will keep you apart from that pretty girl you like so much and she will become the master's, to do anything he wants to do with her. That master will want the pretty ones like Misty. You will curse them, but you will also curse yourself, wishing that you had done whatever you could do to save this farm from them."

My head was swimming. There was no good way for me to think of what Missus told me. Parts of it I had already thought of myself, and all of it sounded very reasonable, and very horrible. Yet giving Caleb up to certain death was unthinkable. I had to fit this all together differently from the way Missus had laid it out so clearly. I truly did not want her to lose her plantation to another Cherokee slave owner. She had been unusually good to us, to me in particular. I had heard stories about other plantations very much like the one she described. If Caleb did not return to explain to the Council that his claiming to own Bandana was nothing more than a boasting slave trying to look big in the eyes of other slaves, maybe she would lose the plantation. What if Missus was lying to me? I couldn't dismiss that possibility. After all, I was lying to her. This was the woman who taught me to read and write. She trusted me with important jobs. She liked me and I liked her. I still lied to her. It wasn't the first time, either. I had lied to her before about Misty's stolen magazine. Why would I expect Missus to be any different? She might just as easily be lying to me now. I thought, if she is lying, she is good at it. The idea that Misty would be at the mercy of a wicked master tortured me worse than the lash. She had found my weakest spot. Misty was now a part of all my plans. I had to protect her if I could. But with Caleb's life? That was the heart of my problem. I was torn between protecting the two most important people in my life. I loved them both; I was loyal to them both. I was being torn apart inside. What could I do to save them both? I had no information to prove Missus's story to be wrong. I had to accept that a new master might take over the farm. My reasoning was leading me to only one way out of this. Then, Missus poked me. I had been sitting silently for quite a while as I thought. She was waiting for an answer and I had to say something. I put her off. "Missus. I'm feeling very poorly." I slumped over and put my head on the table.

She lost her temper and slapped me on the side of my head. "Wake up, boy. I'm telling you I need your help. What do you have to say?"

I pretended not to understand what she had been talking about. "It sounds like you have troubles, Missus, and I'm sorry for you, but I don't know how I can help you."

"You are sorry for me? No, Book Boy. You're a little mixed up. You better start feeling sorry for yourself because if you don't tell me where Caleb has gone off to, today will be the last time I stop the Light-horse lash from coming down on you."

"Please Missus! I don't know where he is! It's true! Don't call back the lash, Missus!"

Missus raised her voice in anger. "You had better change your mind, Book Boy. You better remember who provides for you and takes care of you. You'd be dead without me. I give you a place to sleep. I give you food. I give you clothing. Don't you forget it. Don't you lie to me, boy. Get out of my sight, now, but I expect you to come see me later with a real answer or you won't want to see what's coming for you and the other slaves on this farm. I'm thinking you all have had it too easy for too long."

I carefully lifted myself up and left by way of the kitchen door in the back of the house. Missus saw right through my lies, and it hurt her to think I would choose Caleb's life over her farm. I knew that I would never give in, even if that would bring her anger down on the other slaves. I felt guilty and torn and angry because, whether she kept the farm or not, it would be bad around here. Maybe worse with a new master. I had made up my mind as I left Caleb at Jumping Ben's place. When and wherever Caleb would go, I would go with him. Now, it was more complicated. Now, there was Misty. If I left, there would be no one to protect her, not that a slave boy could do all that much protecting anyway. She was smart, but very sensitive. She craved beauty and harmony. Even with a reasonable Mistress like Missus, she felt smothered by slavery. Misty dreamed of freedom every bit as much as I did, maybe more. Stealing that magazine, which she couldn't even read, was like reaching out for a taste of freedom, a moment of not being in prison. Who knew what an even harsher life would do to my lovely Misty? Then there was the horrible possibility of a new master taking her by force. These thoughts were driving me mad. For her sake as well as for mine, she had to come with us. That was the only answer. Something Misty said jumped into my mind. When she was cleaning my back, she said she was in. She said she was with me. I don't know if she meant keeping up the story of not knowing Caleb's whereabouts, or if she was somehow aware that I was going and she wanted to go with us. To be fair to her, before she could decide such an important thing, she had to know that the dangers to come were real and many. Already, I could feel danger around me. I was constantly on the lookout for a vague something that could suddenly hurt me. Looking back, that feeling probably came, at least in part, from the unexpected lashing. Mostly, it was the fear that every runaway slave had been taught to feel.

As for what was to come, we would just have to guess about what might happen the best we could and make as practical and detailed a plan as possible to account for everything we might encounter. We would need time to think this through, but Webb's Bend was a small town and soon the Lighthorse would get around to questioning Ben about Caleb. They would be able to search everywhere in just a few days. I was a little surprised that I hadn't heard that he'd been arrested already. I went to the slave house and lay down on my stomach, shirtless, my wounds throbbing. There were no windows in the slave house, so I left the door open to let the cool breeze soothe my back. The distant sound of Cotton Hand's deep, rich singing as he worked in a far-off field lulled me to sleep. I dreamed I was standing on the roof of the big house. I could see all of Webb's Bend. Every person and animal, every wagon, every boat, every horse and rider were as clear as if I were right next to them. There was trouble, though. Some parts of the town had a weird light on them that I somehow knew were places where people had died; not just died, murdered. Then I saw Mr. Money Joe walking slowly along the main street. He had a gun in one hand and a book in the other. Every so often, he would hear a noise and point the gun in its direction. Then a slave ran toward him shouting, "Mr. Money Joe! Mr. Money Joe! Missus's been shot! Missus's been shot!" Thick, dark clouds filled the sky and it started to rain. I jumped from the roof to the ground and started running, aimlessly. Then the slave came to me. He shouted, "Misty was sold! Misty was sold!" I grabbed him by the neck and wrestled him down to the wet, slippery grass. "They can't," I moaned. "They can't."

The closing of the slave house door woke me up. I was wet with sweating and shivering because the air was cool. I lay still. Footsteps approached me in the darkened room. "Book," Misty whispered, her lips touching my ear. "Are you asleep, Book? I only have a minute."

I forgot myself and flipped over onto my back to look at her. I stifled the cry of pain and grit my teeth instead, supporting my weight on my elbows. "Misty, I had the worst dream. Missus was dead and you were sold, it was horrible. And there was nothing I could do. It was horrible."

"I'm here. It's alright. I'm here, Book." She kissed my cheek, then my mouth.

I made myself break away from her lips. "There's something I have to ask you, Misty. And tell you. And I need you to answer right now. You have to be very, very sure about it when you answer because there won't be any mind-changing once it all gets going."

Her face quickly turned serious. Even in the dark, barely able to see her form in the few shafts of light that seeped between the boards of the walls, she was beautiful. "What is it?" she said with a mature steadiness that surprised me.

"Most of my life, from the time I was aware that there was a difference between being a slave and being free, I have needed to be free."

She knew just what I meant. "Me too."

"Sometimes the feeling of being a slave has been too much for me, like I was locked in a room with no air, no light. My heart would pound as though I had been running for miles. I would think that I would just jump right out of my skin or die on the spot."

"Oh, Book." She took my hand.

"A long time ago, I made up a game that I would play when that feeling hit me. I would close my eyes and pretend that I was somewhere else, wherever I wanted to be, doing whatever I wanted to do. I was completely free inside. I called it the freedom game. I got really good at it so that I could play it as soon as I needed it. I still do."

Misty smiled sweetly. "I call it the lady game. I pretend that I'm a fancy lady doing anything I please. That's why I wanted the magazine. It had lots of pictures that I could pretend to be." We laughed a little together, realizing that we shared something important and personal.

"The thing is, I always promised myself that someday the freedom game would come true. I didn't know how or when, but I was sure it would. Now I know."

She turned serious again. "What do you know?"

"How I'm going to be free. I'm halfway there already. Yesterday, at the church, I found the courage to speak up and I got a glimpse of what it was like to say no to being a slave. And I went further than that."

"How further?"

"I helped Caleb get away."

She stared at me, stunned. A minute went by. "Book, do they know? Missus? Does she know? Are you alright?"

"Yes, I'm fine and no, she doesn't know. But Misty, Caleb has to get away from here. Far away. If he doesn't, they'll hang him." I took her hands in mine and looked into her eyes. "And this is my chance. I'm going with him." Misty gasped. "And I want you to come."

She pulled her hands from mine. She whispered, "What? How can I? You want me to come? With you?" Misty was afraid to even talk about it. "Away from here? You mean run away? They'll find us, Book. They'll whip us." She took my hands again and squeezed them. "They will kill us."

Nothing she could say could make me change my mind. I had to change her mind. "Just listen for a minute. Here's what Missus told me when she was trying to make me give up where Caleb is hiding. She needs Caleb to say that the Vanners never gave him a horse. That he just bragged about it, but it wasn't true. And if he didn't say it, Missus would probably lose the plantation. If she loses the plantation, one of two things will happen. Either a new master would come and take it over or she would have to sell off the slaves. She said, if a new master comes, he will be harsh, much harder on the slaves than she ever was. The new master," I hesitated for a moment, "would want a pretty girl like Misty." I pointed to her. "He would want you for himself. Do you know what I mean?" Misty said nothing. I asked again. "Do you know what I mean?" Misty nodded. "And if she or the new master sells the slaves, then you and I would be separated forever. Misty, I cannot let any of that happen."

Misty was still for a minute. She looked away. She had to let it all settle in her mind. I was expecting a yes or a no, maybe an 'I don't know'. Softly, she said, "You love me, don't you?" She touched my face.

A shaft of light that had been streaming into the room from an opening between the wall boards suddenly flickered. Another shaft of light flickered. And another. Someone was walking on the other side of the wall. I put my finger on Misty's mouth. "Shh." I whispered, "Someone's outside." Nearly as soon as I spoke those words, the world outside darkened. We heard the boom of thunder and a strong rain began pouring down. The weather in Webb's Bend was known to change quickly. One minute sunny. The next, clouds and rain. Sometimes a storm would get so strong that small pebbles of ice would shoot down from the sky and sting your skin. It could pour down rain while the sun shone, too. I had even heard of a wind so strong it could lift a whole building up to the sky and come crashing down into pieces. This was just a quick, heavy thunderstorm, though. The roof of the slave house was leaking and Misty and I huddled together to wait it out, thinking about our unwanted, unknown visitor outside. The rain lasted only a few minutes, stopping as abruptly as it had begun. The sun once again shot through the wall spaces. The movement we had seen of someone outside had vanished, but the question of who it was weighed on us. Had the person heard us? Did the person come to spy or was it accidental? We had to find out in a hurry. Not sure if we could still be heard, I silently motioned to Misty to go out the door to the left and that I would go to the right. As quietly as I could, I lifted myself up. I almost cried out in pain and caught myself. I cautiously stepped outside to find the muddy earth around the slave house soaked by the flash of rain. We each went in different directions and met by the wall where the flickering light had told us someone was there. I looked down at the ground to see the deep impressions of two feet that had walked in the mud by the slave house. The impressions were now filled with rainwater and it was easy to see the size and shape of the feet that made them. I showed Misty. "Look. Here's where they were walking."

Misty said, "Uh-huh. Those are small feet. Not a little child's, but no shoes on them. Looks like a barefoot slave girl was caught in the rain. Somebody was spying on us, Book. She was trying her best to hear us, too, standing that close to the wall. Through these spaces between the boards, I'll bet she could probably see us, too. I'm scared." Misty touched my arm. She was trembling. "What if she goes to Missus? We have to find her. There's no telling what Missus might do to us if she finds out what we were talking about." We rushed to the corner of the wall, following the direction of the footprints and looked around, but saw no one. Whoever had been there was gone now. "I'd better get back to the house before they miss me. Please find her and stop her." She kissed my cheek and ran off. I figured that I should give Misty a minute to reach the big house before I could be seen starting back there myself. As much as I wanted to look for the spy, even more important was finding out where Missus wanted me to work that day. I didn't get far when I saw a house slave named Millie talking excitedly to Rose. Rose was her usually steady self, but the girl was making a fuss, waving her arms. I looked down at the girl's bare feet. They were covered in not quite dry mud, up to her ankles. As I approached, Millie looked at me. I could see fear come over her face. She tried to run away, but I grabbed her arm.

I got right to the point. "What did you just say to Rose?" I said with my mouth half closed to muffle my anger. Her eyes were wide with fear, but she said nothing. "What did you hear when you were spying on me? You were spying on me, weren't you? Tell me." With each question, I yanked on her arm. Millie was breathing heavily, with a pained look on her face. She said nothing and kept shifting her vision between me and the front door of the house, as though she expected someone to emerge and save her from this grilling. Rose tried to calm things down.

"I saw she was wet and her feet were all muddy," Rose said. "I asked Millie, here, what she was doing, running around out in the pouring rain." She turned to Millie, "Then you got all excited, didn't you? Saying something about you didn't hear anything." To me, Rose said, "I never even asked her if she heard anything. I can only think she must have meant the thunder. That was the only thing there was to hear." Rose put her hand on the girl's head. "Are you afraid of the thunder, girl? Well, it's all over, for now. You had best get back to work. Where do you belong, honey?"

"Is that what you meant? You heard the thunder?" I said, keeping my grip on her arm. She pulled and wriggled to get free, but I held onto her. "Is thunder all you heard? Only thunder?"

"Yes. Yes, that's what I meant. That's all I heard. I swear, I didn't hear anything. I heard thunder. That's what I heard," she said, looking back at the house.

"Where did you get those muddy feet?" I asked. "This is all grassy around here. Where did the mud come from?"

"I don't know!" she screamed sharply and pulled away from me. The scream startled me. I lost my grip and she broke free. Millie ran awkwardly to the big house, her bare feet slipping on the wet ground and causing her to stumble a few times in her haste. Charging up the stairs and through the front door, she slammed it behind her. Ordinarily, she would have to use the back door, for the slaves. The front door was for free, the back door was for slaves. That was the rule. Slaves like Millie always used the back door, unless they had special business to take care of in the front of the house. Millie must have felt that she could use the front door and not be punished for it. For Millie to break that rule, there could be only one reason. She had to be on her way to tell the mistress of the house, Missus, something so important that she would be forgiven for not using the slave entrance.

"Rose," I said, "I think that girl overheard me talking to Misty in the slave house. She may be running to tell Missus what she heard." Rose wasted no time going after Millie, but she had to use the back door which gave Millie a big head start if she was in a race to find Missus. If the girl were to tell Missus any part of what she heard, my plans for Misty and me would be over before they had even begun. After a few minutes of anxious waiting, Rose appeared, pulling Millie by the arm as they walked toward me from the back of the house. Again, Millie broke free, yanking her arm from Rose's grasp. This time she ran out to the field, leaving Rose and me to worry about what damage she had done while inside the house.

Rose walked over to me and spoke quietly. "I'm not sure, Book Boy. She seemed to be going from room to room in the house, sticking her head in each one as though she were looking for somebody, Missus maybe. She didn't find her as far as I can tell, but I don't really know if she'd already said anything. And I still don't know what do you think she overheard you saying. Did you and Misty talk about Caleb?"

"A little. Mostly we talked about us." I hesitated to share everything with Rose. I was getting used to my thoughts and actions being kept secret, not trusting anyone with the whole truth. It was hard for me to do because I didn't like dishonesty. Some people like to keep secrets, they enjoy pretending, making a lie look real. I'm not one of them. If I'm not telling the truth, it makes me feel like there's a hard rock in my stomach. Lately, that's all I seemed to be doing, though, keeping secrets, hiding the truth, telling lies.

I trusted Rose more than anyone else in the whole world, which made me question why I would hesitate to tell her that all this trouble was about my intention to run away. She would be sad to see me go and I didn't want to make her sad. But, that wasn't the reason. Even though I would never want to hurt Rose, she would find out sooner or later and be sad then, anyway. Out of my own sadness at leaving her, I had already planned to say goodbye to her before leaving. Then, I realized that what kept me from telling her was not how she might feel, but what she might do. I hesitated because I was afraid she would try to talk me out of it. She would be very grown up and logical. She would give me a list of all the dangers that would befall me. She would explain to me that I was just a boy and I could never keep up with Caleb. That I would slow him down, force him to make mistakes. That I would be the cause of our eventual capture and whatever terrible events would come after that happened. She might say that I would even be responsible for his death. All of this, I thought, Rose would surely say to me, and convincingly. But, these ideas were really all my own, not Rose's. As of that moment, Rose didn't even know my plan and hadn't actually said a single word about it, so whatever I imagined she would say to me, was really me, saying these things to myself. I saw that it wasn't Rose making me hesitate, it was me. Did I believe any of it to be true? Would I indeed slow Caleb's escape, bringing danger and possible death? And not just for me, either. Misty, too. I couldn't go without her and if Caleb had to travel with the two of us weighing him down, we might very well cause him to be dragged back in chains or killed in the chase. There was more, though. There was Misty. My foolish dream of freedom at all costs was twisting my thinking to the point where I was willing to risk not only Caleb's life and my own life, but Misty's life, as well. Already it seemed to be coming true when Millie may have overheard Misty and me talking about running away. If that got out, Misty could be lashed just for talking about it. She could easily be killed for doing it. She could die trying to run away all because of me and my foolish plans. It was my own guilt that made me hesitate to tell Rose. My guilt and nothing more. I didn't want to admit it to Rose, whose opinion was so important to me. It would be like looking into a mirror and seeing the reflection of a bad person, my reflection, willing to risk the people he loves for his own selfish desires. "Misty doesn't know where Caleb is," I said to Rose. "But we did talk about something else. Something that no one else should know about," I said.

THE FREEDOM GAME

Rose got more information from me with her kindness than any Lighthorse with a whip ever could. She picked up my hand and patted it, saying, "If you tell me, I'll do my best to help you. If you don't want to tell me, I will understand, completely. It's your secret. It's for you to decide, dear."

Her words were so caring, so loving and welcome, after that, my own words just spilled out, as though my head had overflowed. I had as much chance at holding back from her as the water on a waterfall. Still, I found control enough to whisper, practically mouthing the words for her with almost no sound. "I am going to run away with Caleb, and I am taking Misty with me." Rose said nothing. Her face allowed no special emotion. She let go of my hand, turned and walked away as if I hadn't said anything of importance. Of course, she wanted to cry. She didn't cry. She may have wanted to scold. She didn't scold. She wanted to talk me out of it. She didn't talk. She just walked away. Her strength amazed me. Watching from a distance, even a fairly close distance, no person, slave or free, would think that I had just spoken of my decision to take the most defiant, illegal, dangerous path a slave can take - freeing himself from his slavery.

The time had come for me to face Missus and, in doing so, I would find out if Millie had told my secret, or whatever part of it she could. I slowly made my way to the front door of the big house. I was allowed this entrance because I was Missus's special slave, the one who helped her. I was her most trusted slave, above all others. And now I had lied to her. I opened the door and saw them both in the hallway, in front of the business room. It was clear that Millie had finally caught up with Missus and had begun her story. Missus heard me enter the big house and looked at me.

"Come here, Book Boy," she said with no particular emotion. Maybe I was just in time to stop the spy. "Millie was just telling me quite a story and, evidently, it involves you."

"Missus, I don't know what she told you, but that girl lies. She lies all the time. Everybody knows she lies." My denial was too strong.

"She hasn't really told me much of anything, yet. Why are you so jumpy? What are you hiding from me, boy?"

"Nothing. I just know her is all."

"We'll see," Missus said. "Go on, Millie. What did you come to tell me? Out with it." Millie was shaking. She was not only afraid of me, she was also

73

afraid of what other slaves might do to her if she told Missus all she heard. To a slave owner, a runaway slave was a financial loss, a display of weakness and a legal problem. To a runaway slave, being turned in to the master by another slave was unforgivable. Most of the slaves on the Vanner plantation would never look at Millie the same way. She would be scorned for life. Some slaves would try to physically harm her and with me as a witness to what she was about to tell Missus, she couldn't deny what she said. Millie had a difficult choice to make. I wasn't going to make it any easier.

"Millie, I haven't spoken more than two words to you in months," I said. "What could you possibly know about me to tell Missus? Stop wasting Missus's time, girl."

"Book Boy, I sent Millie to see what you were up to and I want to hear her report, so keep your mouth quiet. If anybody is wasting my time here it's you. Now, Millie, I'm going to ask you one more time. You got something to say or not?"

Millie's voice wavered. "Yes Missus. Yes. Well, I, right before it rained, Book Boy was in the slave house."

"I already know that," Missus said.

"And, and, he wasn't alone."

"He wasn't alone? Go on," Missus said.

"I'm sorry, Book Boy. I'm sorry."

"Come on, girl!" Missus was losing her patience. "Who was he with?"

"He was with Misty. I'm sorry, Book Boy. He and Misty were in the slave house together. Alone."

"They were alone? How do you know?"

"Yes. I saw them through an opening between in the wallboards. They were there. Alone. And they were... kissing. I'm sorry, Book Boy."

"And that's it?" Missus said.

"That's it, Missus. That's what I got."

Missus let out a small laugh. Then a bigger one. Then she laughed so hard she could hardly breathe.

"You alright, Missus?" I said.

"I thought you were going to tell me he was with Caleb! He was kissing

Misty, huh?" She started laughing again. "Well, Book Boy, I guess you're growing up, aren't you? You know, I was sure there was something going on between you two, sneaking looks at each other, little jokes and whispers here and there." Even the embarrassment of having my most private business discussed out loud, and laughed at, didn't change the wonderful relief I felt. Our plans were safe, for now. Whether Millie didn't hear, didn't understand what she heard, or decided at the last minute not to tell, the outcome for us was the same. Missus had a good laugh thinking that my sneaking, hiding and plotting were all for the love of a beautiful slave girl and that was fine with me.

"I'm real sorry, Missus. You were right about us. I didn't think we were doing any harm. It was just a kiss," I said. To Millie, I showed how annoyed I was. "Millie, what are you doing, going around spying on people? What's the matter with you, girl? You want trouble with me? Well, you got it."

"Whoa, Book Boy. Take it easy. I asked Millie to keep an eye on you. I didn't know she was going to peep at you through a hole in the wall, but even so, it was me who sent her, so you back off."

"Yes, Missus."

"I half expected to find out that you were hiding Caleb somewhere on my own farm, right under my nose," she said. "That wouldn't have been so funny, would it?"

"No, Missus."

"How is your back?"

"It hurts a lot. I can work though, if you need me."

"Go, rest," she said. "It can all wait till tomorrow. Millie, you come with me." I watched them walk into Missus's business room. I didn't like that there's was more to be said between them. I waited for Millie in the kitchen near the back door. A few minutes later, Millie strolled into the kitchen with a sly smile curling her lips. She swayed her hips teasingly as she walked straight up to me, face-to-face.

"You owe me, Mister," she said. "You owe me big, big, big, my dear Mister Book Boy." She slowly placed the palm of her hand on my chest. "How are you ever going to thank me?" She caught me off guard. I didn't know what to do or say.

"What? Why?" I was blushing, I could feel the blood rush to my face. "What?"

"Well," she said. "I did just save your life. That's all. Don't you think I deserve one little thank you for saving your life?" She moved her face closer to mine. I looked up to see Misty standing in the doorway, her fists clenched, her eyes burning a hole in the back of Millie's head.

"What am I seeing here?" Misty said. "Book Boy, tell me what I'm seeing here."

Millie answered, keeping her hand planted on my chest, "You're seeing a private conversation between two people and you are not one of them. That's what you're seeing." She pushed on my chest moving me backward against the wall.

Misty was furious. "Take your dirty hand off him or I take it off myself."

"Really?" Millie said. "You better get ready to eat those words." Millie was shorter than Misty, but she was heavier and years of hard labor had made her strong. Misty would be no match for her in a fight. I had to stop them.

"Wait. Wait a minute," I said. "Misty, let me explain this." Misty didn't wait. She lunged for Millie and grabbed her head from the back. Millie easily pulled Misty's hands off and spun around, shoving Misty into the table.

"Stop it! Stop it!" I shouted. I managed to get between them, but they threw punches at each other that mostly landed on me. Missus and Tall Bone came running into the kitchen, Missus from the house, Tall Bone from the back door. Seeing Missus, they stopped the fight.

Tall Bone said, "What's going on here?"

"Bone," Missus shouted, "get Misty out of here. Take her to the tree by the slave house and stay with her till I get there."

"Yes Missus," he said. As Tall Bone left with Misty, Missus took Millie to the tree in front of the big house herself. Fighting among slaves would not be tolerated. She had each one of the girls tied to a tree with a rope, one end around the neck, the other end around the trunk of the tree. They were to remain there until Missus said it was enough. It was getting late in the day and I was worried that Misty would need food. Tall Bone told me Missus would let them eat if someone brought them a plate. I volunteered. For me, this changed nothing. If anything, I was more certain than ever that

THE FREEDOM GAME

Misty and I had to go with Caleb. The harshness that Missus threatened was already taking shape and it would only get worse if we remained. I needed to be free of the constant "Yes, Missus" and "No, Missus." I was angry over the punishment she inflicted on Misty and even for Millie. They weren't dogs to be tied to trees. They shouldn't have been fighting, but the answer didn't have to be more pain, more fear. I started to feel some of the hatred that festered in Cotton Hand's thoughts. The hatred made it easier to do what might be necessary for us to change our fates. If we had to fight, if we had to kill our masters, even if they had been kinder than other masters, so be it. I didn't want to kill anyone, but they had chosen this way of living, buying and selling us as property, treating us like animals, getting rich from our work and our pain. Seeing the rope around Misty's beautiful neck and tied to the tree was too much. It was worse than being lashed. Misty was right; I did love her. That love was driving me deeper and deeper into the absolute need to escape, the need for freedom and not just a game in my head. It was time for the freedom game to become real for Misty and me.

Supper time came. I asked Rose to make two plates, one for Misty and one for Millie. Millie usually ate with another group of slaves, but I wasn't sure they would care enough about her to bring food. They might even be too frightened to interfere with her punishment to try. Since the day Bandana was killed, fear was what made this plantation run. I took the first plate to Misty. She was hugging her knees with her back to the tree. Her head was down with her face buried in her knees. I spoke softly. "Misty, here's some supper. Please eat." She didn't move. "You need your strength." I put the plate down next to her. She looked up. She had been crying. Her eyes were red and swollen.

"I'm so sorry for that, Book," she said. "I knew you didn't want that girl. I knew it, but I just got so jealous of somebody touching you like that, I..." I interrupted her.

"Misty. Listen. You were right before. I really do love you. I love you more than anyone or anything in this whole world." I took her hands and kissed them. "We're young. Already, I'm sick of being somebody's property. I'm tired of being treated like a dog. I was lashed this morning. Look at you now. I can't imagine living our whole lives like this and maybe worse. What if they did sell you? Or me? We would never see each other again. Ever. What if a new master really were to take you for his slave to do whatever he wanted with you? Misty, I just can't stand this anymore."

"Hold me, Book," she said spreading out her arms. I dropped to my knees and eased into her embrace. I kissed her, not caring if we were seen. I whispered, "Some of us are going to talk to Caleb tonight. I will come to you after that. Please eat."

"Alright," she said.

I got up and went back for Millie's plate. I found Millie, looking bored, sitting upright with her legs crossed. Millie was excited to see the food. She grabbed the plate out of my hand. "Thank you! I thought I was going to starve out here, tied up like a dog." She filled her mouth with handfuls of food. She said something as she ate. I couldn't understand her. "Millie, swallow and say it again."

"I said, I'm sorry for causing all this trouble. I thought you were interested. You know, in me. Hey, are you interested?"

"No."

"If you're not interested, then why did you bring me this food?" She grinned as if she had discovered my secret feelings for her.

"I felt sorry for you. I felt kind of responsible because I'm the one who Missus sent you to spy on in the first place."

"You know I heard the whole thing between you and Misty, don't you?"

"I guess so. Look, thank you for not telling anyone. It would be a huge problem for us if you did."

"I never said I didn't tell anyone."

I crouched down next to her. "Did you?"

"I didn't tell Missus, if that's what you mean."

"Did you tell anyone else? Anyone?"

"Maybe." She shrank back from me. Afraid of the look in my eye. She tried to look past me. She had changed her story so many times, running from me, pretending she heard and saw nothing, running to Missus, caught telling something, changing her story, threatening to tell. Believing anything she said now would be impossible.

"Who? How many?" With all that happened, she didn't have much time to tell anyone, but even one person running to Missus would be disastrous.

THE FREEDOM GAME

I thought, that person could be turning me in right now. I grabbed her arms and shook her. "Speak, Millie." Tied to the tree, she couldn't get away. She had to deal with me.

"I only told one person and I don't think he understood me anyway. It's alright. You and Misty are alright. There's just one thing."

"What?"

"When you go, I'm going, too."

"No! Are you crazy? I can't take you. With that many we'd never have a chance. We'd be dead for sure."

"I don't think you've got much of a choice, Book Boy." Millie laughed, sure she had me. "You don't want this news to get out, you take me with you." The smile left her face. "Book, I can't stand it here. You know why Missus sent me to spy on you? Because I'm always in some kind of trouble. She thinks I'm so scared of her that she can get me to do anything. She's wrong. I didn't tell on you when I could have. That was part me helping you and maybe a bigger part me not doing her dirty jobs for her. I'm done with this slave life. I want out of here and you're going to get me out. That's right. You, my brainy Book, are my Moses. You will lead me to freedom and the promised land. If anybody can figure out how to get there, it's you, sugar." Her smile returned.

"We'll talk about it later. In the meantime, don't say another word about it to anyone or it won't be the promised land, it'll be to the hanging tree."

"My lips are shut tight. For now."

I left Millie eating happily, dreaming about her coming escape to freedom, all as she remained tied to a tree. The day had been fairly warm, but the November cold was definitely in the air that night. No one had questioned my delivery of food to the prisoners. I wondered, if I brought Misty a blanket, would that be too much interference in her punishment? I'd try to get to her after everyone had gone to sleep. As for me, I was too excited to be hungry. Rose made me eat something anyway. Rose, Tall Bone, Cotton Hand and I all gave each other knowing looks, but said not a single word. We would go to see Caleb when the plantation had settled in for the night. The plans would be forged and I would be one step further to finding freedom. I figured that I would have to do some fancy convincing for Caleb to consent to taking Misty and me with him. I needed to prove that we could be of help to him, that we could make his escape more likely to succeed with us than without us. I didn't see how my usual offering, my ability to read and write, could be of too much importance in the escape, none really. I would have to invent something else. It didn't matter, though, because it was to turn out altogether different from anything I had expected. My back was still painful and would probably be so for days. I went to my favorite tree to stretch out for a little while until it was time to go. The past two days seemed so unreal, almost like a story I might make up to entertain myself. The pain kept reminding me that it was all quite real.

CHAPTER 6

It didn't take long for Caleb to befriend Jumping Ben. The quick but drenching rain that had shown Millie's footprints near the slave house also showed where Jumping Ben and Miss Annie's cabin roof, on the other side of town, was having problems. Miss Annie had done her best to set out containers of various types and sizes to keep the dripping water from combining with the dirt floor to form sticky mud puddles. Caleb, a skilled carpenter, knew just what to do about a leaky roof. He helped with the nearly empty wood pile and the hinge on the shed door that was coming loose, too. He was an expert at fixing and chopping and didn't have to be asked to use his expertise. He liked work, and, seeing a job that needed doing, Caleb was more than happy to dive in. Ben told me later that he offered to help Caleb, but Caleb wouldn't hear of it. So, Ben and Annie just kept Caleb company as he worked. The three of them traded stories about how Webb's Bend had changed over the years, how even though the weather was unusually warm in the daytime, it was turning colder at night, and how we were probably due for more lightning storms. Caleb told them about a strange wind storm he once saw that flattened an entire large house, right before his eyes. Ben called a storm like that unole. He said it was pronounced oo-no-lay. He also thought that another such storm was long overdue. In his opinion, the unole came when people were in conflict with each other, as they were at that moment. The greater the disagreement, the more devastating the unole. Ben said with important Cherokee families trying to bring one another down, and the misery of slaves haunting everything about life in Webb's Bend, this was the time of conflict that brought the unole. Annie dismissed that as silly talk. She didn't believe that the weather had anything to do with what was happening between people. She did say we were due for one, though.

No Light-horse had come to their house searching for Caleb, but I had heard talk between two overseers that a hired posse was forming to find him.

They would be paid by Mr. Money Joe who must have thought Caleb had left Webb's Bend already. That would explain why the Light-horse did not do the house-to-house search I had feared would uncover Caleb's whereabouts within days. This was good news for us. It would give us some room to make plans and get a nice head start on the posse, depending on how fast our feet could get moving. I couldn't contain my excitement. Tonight would decide Misty's and my future and, of course, Caleb's. I was tingling from head to toe, giddy and grinning that my time of freedom had finally arrived. I was a little ashamed that I felt almost grateful to Caleb for his troubles because they presented me with such a splendid opportunity. I wished Bandana were alive, I wished Caleb was not marked for death, I wished I had not been lashed, I wished Misty didn't have to worry about a harsh life, and yet all that sorrow had lead me to this glorious moment, when the people I loved and trusted most in the world were planning to help me escape. They just didn't know it yet, that's all. They thought they were only helping Caleb to escape. Soon they would find out it was for Misty and me, too.

If the four of us left to go to Ben's place all at once, it could attract too much attention from the other slaves. I had the feeling there was already a high level of suspicion. Others must have seen us and wondered what we were whispering about. By now, it was well known that Missus had sent Millie to spy on me, and both Millie and Misty were being punished in plain sight. Stories were being told, mostly fictional, to explain these unusual goings-on. As I was getting ready to go to Ben and Miss Annie's, I wondered if Missus might very well have someone watching me right now. To be cautious, we decided to stagger the times when we would sneak off the plantation. I would go first, then Rose, then Tall Bone, and then Cotton Hand. I gave them exact directions. It wasn't far, but if you missed the turn for Ben's path, especially in the dark, you could get very lost in the woods. The sun was down. It was time for me to go. I kept looking around me, seeing and hearing imaginary spies everywhere. On my way out, I made sure I caught a glimpse of Misty, still tied to the tree. Her eyes were closed and I suppose she was asleep, but I dared not talk to her. I wanted so much to put a blanket on her and tell her how excited I was that we were moving ahead with our plans. I couldn't risk it. The tree was too near the big house and I might be discovered if I got too close. No, the best thing for me to do was to get to Jumping Ben's place as fast and as quietly as I could. I knew the way well, so I managed to make all the right turns while my mind was full of dreams about what our life would be like once we were free. Before I knew it, I was there, standing in front of Ben and Miss Annie's cabin. The door was open slightly and a yellow-orange glow from the fireplace colored the room. I heard a low boom of distant thunder, but there was no rain. Ordinarily, it would have startled me, but the night was so unreal already, it seemed only natural to have strange sounds in the background.

As we had planned, I was the first to arrive. I looked into the open doorway and saw Miss Annie, Jumping Ben and Caleb near the fire, laughing about something. It was clear they had become good friends in this short while. I was glad to see it, but not too surprised. I knew they were all good people who would take a natural liking to the goodness they found in each other. Wolfie, Ben and Annie's dog, was content to lie in his usual place near the fire. At first I wasn't noticed, so I knocked on the door to get their attention. They looked up and smiled. Caleb came right over to me and shook my hand.

"I'm real glad to see you, Book Boy," he said. "I was starting to worry that something bad had happened to you." He clapped his big hand on my back right on my lash wound and I let out a cry of pain. He pulled his hand away quick and stepped back. "What's the matter?"

"Those two Light-horse men came around this morning," I said. "They tried to get me to tell them where you are. But I wouldn't talk. I wouldn't tell them anything. They lashed me a couple of times to get me to talk, but Missus stopped them. Misty cleaned me up, but it does hurt, though. Missus let me rest up so I feel better, but it still hurts."

Miss Annie lifted up my shirt to look at my back. "Mm...mm...mm, what they did to you," she said, shaking her head. "The wound where the whip hit you is open. I have something for that." She reached into the cupboard and re-arranged a few things until she found what she was looking for, a jar of salve. She opened the jar and gently spread a small amount onto the open wound. It immediately felt better. "That should heal faster, now."

"It feels better already," I said, happily.

Caleb came over for a look. "I'm sorry, Book Boy. After I'm gone for a while, I'm sure they will leave you alone."

That was as good a time as any to make my announcement. "Well, Caleb,

I've been doing a lot of thinking about you leaving. A lot of thinking." I was scared to say what was on my mind for fear he would say no. I would not, I could not, accept a no.

"What are you thinking Book?" he asked.

"I'm coming with you."

He laughed. "No."

"With Misty."

Then he spoke like the man in charge of the project, his usual role. "You better change that thinking you've been doing because there is no way you can go where I am going to have to go. And there is no, no, no way your girlfriend can go. The answer is no."

This was going to be harder than I figured. I pressed on. "Look. You'll need us. Nobody can travel alone. It's not safe to travel alone. Who will keep watch when you sleep? And once you get to wherever, you'll need me to read for you, write for you."

"Book Boy, I truly appreciate everything you've done and everything you're doing, but you'd be risking your life and Misty's. It just can't be," he said.

Even though I was getting twisted up inside, this conversation was so important that I forced myself to speak calmly. I needed to act grown up if was going to be trusted. "Maybe you'll see why we have to go with you when you hear the whole story. Missus told me that they had to find you now, because they need you to explain to the Council that Mr. Money Joe never gave you Bandana for your own. If they don't get you to say that, then they could lose everything, since a slave owning a horse is against the law. They would have to sell us off and I would never see Misty again. And a new master might do bad things to Misty, her being a beautiful girl." I was getting too frantic. I needed to make myself understood. I needed to show him how much this meant to me. "I couldn't stand that, Caleb, I just couldn't. I think of her at the mercy of a master who forces himself on her and I can't control what I might do. I wouldn't even care what happened to me. Do you know what I'm saying?" I looked to Annie and Ben and then back to Caleb. They had never seen this side of me. It was new to me, too. "Also, Caleb, you know how I always wanted my freedom. I dream about freedom every day. Now I have a chance at being free I never thought I would really have. This is my chance, with friends to help me."

"Friends? What friends are you talking about?" Caleb said.

"Oh," Another shock was coming and there was no way out of it. "Well, Rose, Tall Bone and Cotton Hand are on their way here."

Caleb's voice got louder. "You told them I was here?" Ben and Annie looked at each other as if they were sure they made a mistake taking Caleb into their home.

"I had to. But it's alright. We can trust them. They will help us." I waited a minute for it to sink in. "The one I'm really concerned about is Millie."

"Who is Millie?" they all said, practically at once.

"She's a kitchen slave Missus sent to spy on me. I hardly know her. She overheard me tell Misty that I was planning for us to go with you. Don't worry, she doesn't know where you are. But I think she might have told some other slaves that Misty and I are going to run away. I don't think she told Missus. After all, Missus had Misty and Millie tied to trees as punishment."

"Punishment for what?" Caleb said, starting to get used to being surprised by me.

"They were fighting," I said.

"What were they fighting about?" Caleb asked.

"I guess me." I changed the subject. "It doesn't matter, though. It's all settled and besides, we'll be gone soon. Right?"

At that moment, Tall Bone, Cotton Hand and Rose entered the room through the open door. I didn't expect to see them all at once. "I thought we were all coming separately?"

Rose answered, "We were afraid of getting lost in the dark and we were too excited anyway. Caleb, I'm glad to see you looking well. Your new friends are taking good care of you." She turned to Ben and Annie. "Thank you. You are wonderful people. Thank you so much."

The warmth of Rose's thanks helped Annie set aside her fear. Feeling she could trust Rose, Annie put her hand out for Rose to shake. "I'm Annie Carter. This is my husband, Jumping Ben Carter."

Rose took her hand, smiling. "I'm Rose. This is Tall Bone and this is Cotton Hand." Tall Bone shook hands with Ben and Annie.

Cotton Hand hesitated, at first, saying, "I don't think you want to shake my hand, Miss. It's kind of messed up." He looked at the floor, ashamed.

"Oh, I don't mind," Annie said with a gentle smile, graciously taking his scarred hand in hers. Cotton Hand actually smiled back, a facial expression he rarely displayed.

Caleb was happy, too, that we had all come. "I didn't think I would see any of you friends again. My life has taken a strange turn. And Book Boy's announcement that he intends to go with me and bring Misty along for the ride is making this even stranger." Tall Bone started laughing. "I know, it's funny," Caleb said. "What a crazy idea!"

Then Rose started laughing, too. "Well, maybe not that crazy," she said. "We're going, too."

Caleb stood up. "What?" he shouted.

Rose explained for the group. "Calm down, Caleb. We all decided. This is our moment, too. Yes, you were forced into it and we weren't. But that doesn't mean we can't choose for ourselves. Admit it. We have all thought of running away one time or another, haven't we? We all want our freedom, don't we? Wished for it. Prayed for it. The only thing standing in the way is being afraid of getting caught." She continued slowly and carefully, trying to explain her logic clearly. "And why is it so few runaways really make it to their freedom? We all talked about it. You see, if we go as a group, together, we can do it. The problem is, when slaves run away one at a time, they are easy targets for a slave catcher. It's easy to sneak up on one person. But, if we help each other as a group, the slave catchers would leave us alone. They would be too afraid of us and they would rather stick to looking for one runaway by himself. When you look at it that way, running makes good sense." The group was pleased with Rose's speech. She smiled confidently, proud of the words she had spoken.

Caleb stroked his chin, thoughtfully. He looked into the fire, trying to find the right words. "Rose, that was good. I understand. And you're right, single runaways are easy to pick off. And you're right that you all want to run away, but were afraid until now. Like I said, that's all good. What I think is that if we go as a group, you, Bone, Cotton, Book, Misty and me, that would be a big enough deal for Mr. Money Joe Vanner to hire himself a posse of slave catchers to come after us. There will be plenty of Cherokees, Choctaws and whites who would very much like to get whatever pay and reward that's going to be offered for us, alive or dead." Their smiles fell. Caleb continued, "Now, I'm not saying this escape can't be done. You're all very important to me and I can think of nothing I would like better than for all of us to be free, together. So, I'm not saying flat out no. What I am saying is that we have to have a clear workable plan. If we go off just running wild, they'll be on us before we get out of Webb's Bend." The group, including me, took Caleb's words as a yes. We started cheering and Ben put his hand on as many of our mouths as he could with only two hands, reminding us that this was a secret meeting.

I considered it settled that we were all going and that we were in need of a plan, so I had something to say. "I have a plan. Well, most of a plan. Part of a plan."

Caleb grew impatient. "Well, what is it? Spit it out."

"Alright. Not too long ago, Miss Annie got a letter from her sister. She lives in a place called Texas. In the letter, she mentioned there were slaves, but they would sometimes run away, free as a bird, never to come back."

"I remember that letter," Annie said.

"Slaves run away all the time. So what?" Tall Bone said.

"But it seems that a lot of these slaves not only run away, they get away. That's because they go to another country, nearby, called Mexico. And in Mexico, there is no slavery! Slavery is against the law!" The group practically gasped. "You can't get caught if nobody wants to catch you. I say, Mexico is where we should go." I think I was grinning. I wanted to jump up and down and laugh and be proud to have found just the right place for us. The group hugged me and patted me at told me how smart I was. It was like a beautiful dream. I felt fearless. I knew we could take on the whole world if we had to.

Then Cotton Hand spoke. "How do we get there? I mean, where is Mexico?"

They all looked at me. "I don't know, exactly speaking." They moaned their disappointment. "But it can't be too far if it's near Annie's sister, right?" I looked at Annie. "Right?"

"I think it took my sister about three weeks to get to Texas," Annie said. "Ben helped her move." All eyes shifted to Jumping Ben. He slowly walked over to the fireplace and chose a short firebrand from the burning wood. He blew out the bit of fire that burned at the end of the stick and cooled it off. Then he walked slowly to the whitewashed wall, illuminated by the yellow glow that caught most of the room, but made this wall brighter than the rest of the room. He used the charred end of the stick to make an X near the top right corner of the wall.

Miss Annie sprang to her feet. "Ben Carter, what in the world do you think you're doing to my white wall?" she demanded. That was the first time I ever heard Jumping Ben's last name. "Have you gone crazy?"

"It's okay Annie," Ben replied, soothingly. "After I'm finished, I'll take a dishrag and wipe it all away. Good?" He winked at her.

Annie giggled. "Well, so long as you wipe it all off. All of it, you hear?"

"Yes, ma'am, I will. All of it." Ben turned to the group. "That X is where we are here. I'm going to use this wall to draw a picture map of where you want to go and how to get there. I've been down there and back when I helped move Annie's sister to Texas and I know the way pretty well. It's far. A long ride on horseback. On foot, I can't say. Even with supplies, you'll be hungry and thirsty. There are some trails part of the way, but, to avoid towns and slave catchers, you'll have to make some new trails. It'll take you through the Creek Nation and then the Choctaw Nation before you get to the Texas border at the Red River. Neither Creek nor Choctaw are friendly to runaway slaves. If they catch you, they'll try to return you for a reward or sell you outright. Might even keep you if they have a need. If the reward is dead or alive, they might just kill you to save them the trouble." There was absolute silence as we listened to the man who had been where we wanted to go. "Before I go on, there's something you have to know about the border. It used to be that when you crossed the Red River into Texas you were in Mexico. That's because Texas was part of Mexico. Lately, that's all changed. General Sam Houston made war on Mexico and Texas is now the Republic of Texas. Texas is its own country with its own laws. And it's a lot more like the United States than it is like Mexico. General Sam Houston used to live in the Cherokee Nation as our brother. In fact, we call him by a Cherokee name, The Raven. The Raven is an American who became a Cherokee, who became a Texan. I've spoken with him many times and I can tell you he never really liked slavery. That doesn't matter though, since the citizens of Texas, once they were free of Mexico, made slavery legal. So even when you cross the border to leave the Indian Territory, you'll still be in danger there. You'll have to travel through part of Texas to get to Mexico where there is no slavery." We whispered to each other, making sure we understood about the difference between Texas and Mexico. Then, everyone's eyes were back on Ben. No one said a word as Ben started drawing some lines on the wall. "Are you with me so far?" We all nodded. "Good." He returned to the wall. "You all know the Arkansas River. That's over here." He pointed to a vertical line he had drawn down the right side of the wall. "If you come to the Arkansas, you're headed east and that's the wrong direction. You want to keep going south. South. Only south. At least until you cross the Red River. But you'll have to cover a couple of hundred miles. Here's how it will go. First you come to Dirty Creek. Mostly mud this time of year." He drew a horizontal line across the wall. "That's Dirty Creek. Shouldn't be too bad to get past it. Then you'll come to the Canadian River. The Canadian can get wide and could be deep in spots. You have to look for a good part of the river to cross. And there are places where crossing is much easier. I can remember one part of the river where there's a big island in the middle of the water. The island is so wide that it takes up most of the river in that one spot. You wade through from the north bank to the island, walk over the island and wade out to the south bank. That's a good place. You have to look for a good place like that." He stopped drawing and said, "Oh, and whenever there's water, there can always be quicksand nearby.

Rose interrupted. "What's quicksand? Does it make you go quicker? Maybe that's better because we're surely in a big hurry to get out of this place." Everyone laughed.

"I'm afraid not, Rose." Ben turned serious. "Quicksand is a kind of wet earth that, when you step in it, it sucks you in and slowly takes you under. Horses, hogs, cattle, people, anybody can get stuck in quicksand. Anybody can disappear into the quicksand. Once you're in, the only way to stay alive is to be dragged out of it by somebody else. You'll need plenty of long length rope to throw to the stuck person if that happens." We got the message that quicksand was no joke.

"Once we cross over the Red River into Texas, then where do we go?" Caleb asked.

"The Red River is about as far as I went with Annie's sister," Ben answered. He took a second burning stick, blew out the flame, winked again at

Annie, and continued drawing as he spoke. "But I can tell you that there is a famous trading trail that follows the Red River west through Texas. It's called the Chihuahua Trail because it leads to Chihuahua, Mexico. When the Red River ends, the trail runs southwest, still in Texas, until you come to the Rio Grande. That's the border of Mexico. When you cross the Rio Grande from Texas, you are in Chihuahua, Mexico. And that's how you get to Mexico."

We were overwhelmed. We would need wagon full of luck and strength of an ox to make this journey to freedom. Under the best conditions, the trip would be difficult. But we would be chased by a posse and slave catchers on top of it. If they caught up with us we would have to fight. "We need to be prepared to fight hard," Cotton Hand said with a special delight.

"To fight everyone who might want to catch us and kill us, we could use a small army," Rose said. As she finished her sentence, we heard talking, coming from outside. Ben had closed the door before drawing the map. The cabin had no windows, but from the space between the door and the wall, I could make out the flickering of a flame.

"Quiet," I said. "There are people outside. I think they have a torch." Ben took his loaded musket from the rack on the wall. He motioned for us to move to the opposite side of the room where we would not be seen when he opened the door. My first thought was that the Light-horse had found us. My heart sank. Just as we were making progress, everything would be snatched away in an instant. But the sounds were more of regular people, people who knew and liked each other. There were young voices, too. It was impossible, yet they sounded familiar. Slowly, Ben cracked open the door, his musket preceding him. As he did, the chatter outside stopped instantly. He looked at us, then peeked out, gripping his cocked musket, ready to shoot. What he saw made him point the musket to the ceiling and fling the door wide open. The mysterious chatter had come from about twenty slaves who had followed us to Ben and Annie's. Misty and Millie were at their head, leading the way by torchlight. Their fellow slaves had freed them from the punishment trees so that they could come along. The fiery torches were like close-up stars, come to life against the black woods. I remember Misty's shining, searching eyes, finding me in the warm, glowing room. To see her there, to see everyone there, I could hardly speak, the emotion in me spilling over. We all had the same dream of freedom and would risk everything to make it real.

"We're going, too," Millie said waving her arms at the crowd of people that had gathered. "All of us. Please. We want to go."

The inside group walked through the door and stood in front of the new group. Caleb was the first to speak. "I'm not sure you understand. This will be a very long, very difficult journey. The chance we can find our way to freedom is small. There's a much bigger chance that we may all die trying. The slave owners will send a posse to catch us. They will find us and we will have to fight them. With guns. With knives. With our hands. We will have to help each other, defend each other."

"Where are you going?" said a voice from the crowd.

I answered, "We'll go south. We will try to find our way to a place called Mexico. It's a country where there is no slavery, where we can be free. Our friend, Mr. Jumping Ben, has been most of the way there." I pointed him out, "Mr. Ben has kindly drawn us a map, but since none of us have ever been there, we could quickly find ourselves lost and alone, easy prey for slave catchers. Only come if your heart is prepared for the most difficult thing you will ever do. Has anyone here been to Mexico?" There was no reply from the group, only a fearful silence. "How about Texas? Anyone?"

Rose said, "The truth is, Book Boy, I could hardly follow the map that Mr. Ben drew. I don't know how we would even begin."

Tall Bone agreed. "The map was good, but I know on the ground we could get lost in a day. It could all be over in a day. With this many, it would be even harder." We had gone from hopeful to hopeless in a matter of minutes. We stood there looking at each other for answers that would not come.

Ben raised both his hands in the air and said, "Wait. Everybody, wait here." We obeyed as he went back into the house. I heard him talking in a low voice with Annie. He and Annie emerged from the house. Ben was half smiling, Annie looked sad, as if she were about to lose everything she loved. Ben spoke to us. "I have decided that, if you wish it, I will go with you and show you the way as far as the Red River at the Texas border." He looked at Annie. She was trying to hide her face with her hand, but Ben could tell that she was crying. The thought of Ben placing himself in such danger over-whelmed her. Ben continued, "Then I will come home and you will go on to Mexico." Rose ran to him and kissed his hand as Caleb shook his other hand. I hugged Annie and whispered, "Thank you. Thank you. We will all thank you forever."

Tears streamed down her face. "I will try to be happy for you, but I am not happy for Ben and me," she said.

The people whispered to each other, unsure of what was happening or what they should do next. Their eyes turned to Caleb, just as they had looked to him for wisdom in the past. He had never turned them away and never would, especially now when he felt responsible for raising their hopes. Hiding his own uncertainty, Caleb placed himself in front of the crowd. "Mr. Jumping Ben, the most generous man I know, has offered to show us the way on our journey to freedom. He has been there before and knows about how to survive in the wilderness where we will be traveling. We gladly accept his help and we will follow his wise advice. We thank him with all our hearts. May God bless him and his wonderful wife, Miss Annie." Some people made their thanks heard with cheering, but were quickly hushed to keep from arousing suspicion. We stood quietly for several minutes, wondering how to proceed. Eyes wide, we knew there was a lot to be done but not how to begin. Caleb again took charge. "This is a large group for traveling and each of us must to do his or her share to make our journey a success." He paused as though he were listening to a voice inside of him. "Alright. Here is what I think we should do. We first prepare for the journey with the proper supplies. We will have to do what we can to make it difficult for them to follow us. And we must ready ourselves for a fight. We will leave this place before daybreak as quick as we can. Whatever job you may be asked to do, we are all depending on you to do it well. Every single one of us is important. Do your work as fast and as quietly as possible." Caleb looked over the people assembled before him, to assign them what to do. He gave his instructions as well as any general ever lead an army into battle. "Rose, you're in charge of food and other necessaries. Pack it so that it will travel well. Get it from anywhere you can, Grady's, the big house kitchen, anywhere, but don't wake anybody. Only talk when you have to, and then only whisper." He turned next to Tall Bone. "Bone, take some men and go to Grady's. You'll need hammers. You take the head of the hammer and wrap it up well with thick cloth. You can find some in the store, but it has to be thick enough so that the hammer won't make too much noise hitting nails. It'll just make kind of a thud. You each take a bag of nails. Then go back to the Vanner place. Quiet, so no one wakes up, even for a minute. Use those padded hammers to nail shut every first floor window and every outside door of the big house and each of the overseer's houses. The better you seal them up, good and tight, the more trouble they will have getting out in the morning. By the time they break free, we should be long gone." He looked to Cotton Hand. "Cotton, you know about guns, don't you?" Cotton Hand nodded. "Well, we need guns. Go to Grady's and take them all. And all the balls and powder and whatever else makes them shoot. Get every gun they've got. Whatever guns you take from them are guns they can't shoot at us. We have to make it as hard for them to fight us as we can." Then he looked at me. "Book, you come with me. We're in charge of rounding up the horses. I want all the Vanner riding horses, every single one. That way, old Money Joe will have to walk for help once he breaks out of his house." We laughed at the thought of the master of the Vanner plantation fuming and cursing, forced to walk, to beg his enemies for help, outsmarted by his own slaves. Of course, the real reason for wanting all the horses, even ones we couldn't use, was to give us more time to get away. It sure was a funny notion, though. "And we need a strong covered wagon for the supplies and for the children to ride in. One with new wheels that won't break going over rough ground."

Ben spoke up. "Caleb, a supply wagon is already sitting in front of Grady's. I watched it being unloaded today and the driver is spending the night at the William place. The team was fed and they're asleep standing nearby."

"Perfect," Caleb said. He again raised his hands to gain the attention of the entire group of hopeful faces, about to attempt the impossible. "Cotton, you and your crew are in charge of putting up our supplies onto the wagon. Now. Everybody, listen. When you take what you need for our journey to succeed, there's something I want you to remember." He suddenly stopped talking and his eyes slowly moved from person to person as though he were trying to look each one directly in the eye. "We are not thieves. We have no money to pay for what we need because they do not pay us for the work we do. But we should take only what we need and no more, no less. Yes, we are owed much, much more than whatever we could possibly carry away with us. But we are not thieves." Caleb softened his expression. "What we are... is free. As of this very minute, I declare us free. We don't belong to anyone. We are not property, we are people. Because we are free, we will act as free people. We will do what we can for ourselves. You are working for yourself now. You work not to make the master rich. That kind of work is over for you. We work to build a new life for ourselves and for our children and their children. Come to the wagon in front of Grady's the minute that you're job is finished. We must leave well before sun up. The soonest we can. Do not be late. We can't wait for anyone. If you don't want to be left behind, be there. Alright then, to work. Fast, quiet and Godspeed."

Everybody's first stop was Grady's because nearly everything to get started would be there. Tall Bone lead the way with his hammer crew. He found what he needed right away and passed the hammers out. The men took soft, thick cloth and carefully wrapped the hammer heads as Caleb had told them, then tied the cloth to the hammer with twine to keep it from falling off. With bags full of nails, Tall Bone returned to the plantation to silently make prisoners of the master and his men in their own homes, while they slept.

Cotton Hand was upset. He waved his muscled arm to get Caleb's attention as we were busy getting rope for the horses. "Hey, Caleb," he called, trying not to be too loud.

"What? I don't have time," Caleb said while cutting lengths of rope that would be long enough to lead one horse while riding another one.

"The only guns I can find are these odd-looking ones in this crate. Book Boy, what does this say?"

I looked over to where Cotton was standing. He held up the crate for me to see the words printed on the side. I told him, "It says, Colt revolver hand guns. And the crate next to it is the ammunition."

"Well, if that's all there is, pack the two crates in the wagon," Caleb ordered.

"But I never saw a gun like this. I don't even know how to load it," said Cotton Hand.

Caleb answered as we walked out of the door. "Just pack it. We'll figure it out later. Book Boy will read us the writing on how to do it." Maybe my reading was going to come in handy again, but things were moving so quickly now I could hardly believe it. By torchlight, lantern or in total darkness, twenty-five souls worked as fast as they could to change their destinies. Our work was different from any other work we had ever done in our lives. Ours was the work of free people who had decided for themselves to choose freedom over slavery. This was not freedom sometimes granted by a generous, big-hearted master for a favorite slave from his deathbed. In my freedom game, I had used images of freedom to soothe my troubled heart. This was not that kind of freedom, either, appearing with little effort and then vanishing from my mind, returning me to a slavery I had never truly left behind. This freedom we decided. We would to work to keep it, nourish with our cunning and defend with our courage. Just two days ago, in front of the church, reading the paper that ordered the Light-horse to arrest Caleb, I felt it for a moment. Now, I will never be anything but free again. Maybe I always was.

"Book Boy, come with me." Caleb handed me some of the coiled lengths of rope he took from Grady's. "We've got some horses to rustle," he said with a delight I had never seen in him before. In a leather holster at his side, where he once carried tools to build, he kept the long, sharp knife he had used to cut the rope. Caleb the mechanic, the carpenter, had become Caleb the rustler and warrior. Could I become such a warrior? I had read stories of ancient knights who fought with honor for a worthy cause. They were willing to sacrifice, face danger, perhaps death, not for sport, not to impress. They believed that their fight was more important than themselves. Could I be such a knight? I wasn't sure, but I was determined to try. As we felt our way through the darkness, I looked up at the wide night sky. I didn't know what the sky looked like in other places, but here, in Webb's Bend, the clear fall air allowed every star to sparkle its best sparkle, and the moon to shine its brightest bright. We were like those stars and that moon, shining our brightest bright, daring to cast away everything we had been taught about who we were and what our lives were for, from our earliest recollections to this sparkling minute. There was no going back to who we were, as familiar and oddly safe as it seemed. My purpose was not simply to obey my master's every whim and command. I needed to have a reason to do whatever I did, my own reason. In that night, our work changed us forever. In it, I became a warrior for freedom.

We smelled the horses before we saw them, and following the scent, we found the corral. These were around twenty of the master's fastest riding horses, not the thick, muscled farm beasts. These racers were exactly the ones we wanted to capture. Caleb was pleased. "Find the gate, but don't open it yet. We'll saddle as many as we can first. Then, we'll tie one to another with the ropes, like a chain. That's the way we'll lead them straight to Grady's. Horses understand strength. Not here," he pointed to the muscle of his arm, "in here," he pointed to his heart. "If he thinks what you want is stronger than what he wants and then he'll follow what you want. Usually. But, if you're not sure what you want the horse to do, he'll know and you best leave off until you are sure. Whatever you do, don't scare them. Then they'll make a lot of noise that we do not need at all." In the main, the horses cooperated. There was some snorting and nickering, but not enough to make anyone wake up and notice. I was thinking about how Caleb must have felt among the horses in that corral. It was where Bandana would have been tonight if the Light-horse had kept better control of his pistol. These horses knew Caleb and Bandana; they saw Caleb just about every day. That must be why this went so smoothly. As he worked with each one, he would say something soft and pet the horse between the eyes. I'm sure he was thinking of the friend that was taken from him so suddenly. Before this, I never had much to do with the horses. My only traveling was from the plantation to town and back again, and always on foot, unless I rode with Missus in a wagon. I'd seen enough riders to have an idea of what to do, but, having only been on a horse myself a few times, the idea of riding hundreds of miles made me consider riding in the wagon as much as possible.

"Caleb." He turned to look at me. "I'm not much for riding horses. I'm a slave in the big house."

"Number one. You're not a slave anymore."

I smiled. "Right. But riding..."

"Number two. You'll be a great rider in no time. I'll show you whatever you need to know and you'll get more practice than a cowboy on the trip we'll be taking." As he attached the last horse to the rope chain he brought me to the second horse in line. "This one is yours. Her name is Marigold. She's gentle, strong and fast. Put your foot there, pull up and swing your leg over." I hesitated. "Misty is waiting, boy. Heh, heh, heh," he laughed. I did as he said and there I sat, teetering, atop Marigold. She was a big horse and I felt very high up and, in a way, important. Caleb mounted the lead horse and kept him to a walk to keep the other horses calm and manageable. The horse chain worked perfectly. They marched, one following another along every road and turn, neat and sweet as you please, reaching Grady's without incident. As we rode, Caleb gave me quick lessons on how to ride. I did my best to listen, but my head spun with the excitement of our adventure.

There was muffled cheering, a ripple of excitement rather than sound that passed through our bodies, as our column of horses was seen coming down the road. Caleb asked Rose if everyone had returned and was told that all the preparations were complete, except for Tall Bone who was still working on sealing up the houses with his crew. We looked into the wagon to find skillfully packed food and supplies for the journey, leaving ample space for a few of the youngest as passengers. It was decided that Rose would be the wagon driver. The rest would ride horses. Those who were unable to control a horse would ride with someone else. The remaining horses would be tethered to the rear of the wagon. We were ready to depart.

Misty worried out loud about Tall Bone. "All that hammering might have been too loud. Maybe would should have just gone without all that. Maybe Missus woke up and the master is on his way here right now with his men."

Millie chimed in, "She's right. We should leave right now."

"No." I said. "We have to give him time. The odds are against us, so every advantage, like closing up the houses, could make the difference. Besides, Caleb and I took all of the master's riding horses. We have to wait for Bone."

"We wait," Caleb said. "But, if he's not back in a few minutes, Book Boy will go see what's..." With that, Tall Bone and his men appeared out of the darkness.

"It's done," Tall Bone said, laughing. "Ha ha. I only wish I could see them scurrying around like cotton rats, trying to get out tomorrow morning. Ha ha. We nailed every door and window shut tight." We all laughed to think of our hated master, a prisoner, unable to escape his own home.

Rose said, "It was a miracle that you weren't found out. A miracle from Heaven. Praise the Lord."

Tall Bone said, "Amen, Rose, Amen." That's how our journey began on the dark, cool morning of November 15, 1842.

CHAPTER 7

Caleb invited everyone to choose a horse for the journey. In the dark, it was hard to detect any differences between the animals, and most just mounted the nearest one. The decision was made to keep Caleb's quiet-moving horse train together, this time with the former slaves in the saddles, at least until we were well out of town and far from any homes near the road that might be disturbed by the sound of galloping hooves on the hard ground. Positioned at the rear of our column, Rose took up the reins of the wagon. She'd driven for Missus many times before and she had the strong hands and arms to do the job. Caleb thought she would also serve as the best supervisor of our supplies. Her good judgment to dole out what, when and to whom was valuable because we couldn't afford to waste anything, not one drop of water, nor one strip of dried beef. A wilderness of unknown size and hazards awaited us, and though we eagerly embraced it, surviving might very well depend on how those supplies were used.

So we set out from Webb's Bend , slowly at first, taking great care to leave undetected in the early morning darkness. The pale pink dawn began to light the sky. As the stars faded away, the sun was an eye of brilliant gold to our left. That meant we were heading south. With Ben leading us, there was no need for me to keep track of such things. Still, it was reassuring to have the sun remind me that all was well. It was light enough to see that we were making good progress, putting distance between us and Webb's Bend. I counted twenty-five of us, including the children in the wagon. We had definitely ridden beyond any settlements. No cabins, no farms. I could see nothing but flat, nearly treeless prairie on all sides. Caleb decided that we could remove the tethers, undoing the horse chain to pick up the pace of our escape. We were on some kind of trail; I couldn't call it a road, more like a well-worn horse path. The wagon was the slowest part of our group as the riders, now free of the tethers, separated into a much looser, faster pack, placing the slower moving wagon last in line. Caleb was right about riding, I thought. I was getting pretty comfortable atop Marigold and ready to test my new skill. I had been riding toward the back with the wagon. I kicked my heels into Marigold's flanks, the way Caleb showed me, and, all at once, I felt like I was flying. I sped past horse after horse. I was coming up to Caleb and Ben. I tried to slow down, but Marigold wanted to run and I flew right past them, unable to stop. I had no notion what to do. I could hear Caleb yelling for me to stop, but Marigold was in charge. I was just clinging to her, trying my best not to fall off.

"I can't stop! I can't stop!" I kept shouting.

"I'm coming," Caleb shouted back. His horse galloped alongside my left. He grabbed one rein and gently drew Marigold's head to the side. That slowed her down to a walk. I must have looked very scared. "Are you alright?" he asked.

"I think so," I said timidly.

Caleb laughed. "What happened?"

"I wanted to see if I could go fast."

"Well, now that you know you can, don't," Caleb said, thinking it was all funny. "Don't worry. You'll get the hang of it." He patted Marigold's neck. "Won't he, girl?"

"Soon we will come to Dirty Creek." Ben told Caleb. "See those trees up ahead?"

"Is it hard to cross?" I asked.

"The water is not very deep," Ben replied. "But we'll have to find a place between the trees for the wagon to squeeze through. To cross it you do have to go down a steep bank. That shouldn't be a problem for the horses, but we have to watch out for the wagon and be ready to help slow it going down. We may also have to drag it coming up on the other side."

"I think I'll go back to the wagon," I said.

"No. Stay up here with me for a few minutes," Caleb said. "I want to talk to you about something."

"What is it?"

"So far, there's been no sign that we're being followed. I guess they had a hard time getting out this morning." We laughed. "I wish I could have seen it. Anyway, sooner or later they will come for us and there will be trouble. Shooting trouble."

"I'm afraid I know even less about guns than I do about horses."

"We're going to fix that. But before anybody starts shooting, we have to figure out how to use the guns Cotton put in the wagon."

"You mean you don't know about guns either?"

"That's not it. I'm a pretty good shot. At least with a regular pistol," Caleb said.

"These pistols aren't regular?" I said.

"Neither Cotton, Bone nor I have ever seen anything like it. It's something new. There's a fat loading part that's different from any gun I ever saw."

"I told you, I don't know about guns. What can I do?"

"We got them just the way they were delivered to Grady's. The guns are all packed in one crate. The ammunition is in another. But there's a book. I'm guessing the book is how to load and fire the gun."

"And you want me to read the book."

"You got it, my educated friend." He clapped me on the back, forgetting my lash wounds. It almost knocked me off of Marigold.

"Ow!" I yelped.

"Sorry." Caleb continued. "We can't afford to take any time to stop riding until tonight. But while it's daylight, you can read it and tell us about it. Then, tonight, we'll load the guns and be ready for whatever comes."

As I nodded in agreement, Ben called for everyone to stop riding. He turned his horse to face us. "Everybody, listen. We're coming to Dirty Creek. Those of you on horseback, dismount and walk your horse over, one at a time and wait for the others on the south side. Rose, I think I found a good place for you to cross with the wagon. Follow me."

We all did as Ben said. As promised, he had found just the right part of the creek for the wagon, with wide a enough space between the trees and fewer rocks in the water. Even so, one of the wagon wheels was caught, stuck in the thick, slimy muck on the creek bottom. Rose did her best to urge the animals on. When that didn't work, a few of the men waded in and pushed the wheel forward as the horses pulled. Finally the wagon passed through and soon we were all safely on the other side.

Ben pulled his horse up to where Caleb and I were riding. "We're in Creek Nation territory, now," he said.

"Is that a good thing or a bad thing?" Caleb asked.

Ben raised his eyebrows. "Well,'" he said, "Creeks own slaves, too. And they take their own slave runaways very seriously. There are big rewards for slave catching. If they catch you, they might return you to Money Joe for a reward...or they might sell you... or they might keep you as their own slaves. I reckon you're definitely not out of danger just because you've made it out of Cherokee land."

Ben scared me into action. "I'd better have a look at those guns, now," I said. "We might be in need of them soon."

I turned Marigold around and waited for the wagon to catch up with me. When it arrived, I told Rose, "Caleb wants me to read something in the wagon."

She pulled up the team of horses to a complete stop. "Glad to have you on board," she said in her usual, cheerful way. "Tie your horse to the back of the wagon and climb on in." I did as she said, almost losing my balance as she started moving again on the uneven terrain. I wove my way through the children and supplies in the spacious covered wagon. I finally found the crates that held the weapons and ammunition. I pried open the one marked ammunition, thinking it would have instructions on preparing the gun for firing. Sure enough, a thick booklet, complete with pictures, lay right on top. I figured this would take a while, since I didn't really know much about any weapons. It turned out that these guns were so new and different, nobody knew much about them. They were called Paterson Revolvers, one revolver in each of six fancy wooden boxes in the gun crate. Only six guns seemed like it would hardly be enough to defend ourselves, but the thing that was so different about them was that you could load five shots at a time. Even more important was that you could fire those five shots one right after the other without having to reload. Every other gun I, or anyone else, had ever seen had to be re-loaded after each shot that was fired. Reloading took precious time, especially in the fast-moving situations where these guns would have to be used. I recalled the fear in the eyes of the Light-horse who came to arrest Caleb when he realized that his one pistol shot had been spent accidentally killing Bandana. That Light-horse had no time to reload before the mob would get him, so he ran away instead. A five-shooter pistol, like the one I was reading about, would have made quite a difference that day against us and I guessed it would make just as big or bigger difference in our favor. I studied the booklet carefully. Loading required a carefully ordered series of tasks involving something called a five-chamber cylinder, but if all of the necessary supplies were handy and if two people worked as a loading team, the gun could quickly be made ready to fire off another cylinder of five shots.

We rode through most of the day without seeing a single soul, but the horses were tiring, and so were the people who had not gotten any sleep the night before. The day had been unusually warm for this time of year, and we drank up at least half of our water supply during that one day's ride. Thankfully, Jumping Ben led us off the trail to a good, secluded spot where we could make camp for the night. There was grass for the horses and water for everyone to drink. As the setting sun turned the whole world gold, we ate, drank and settled in to rest.

"Book, please sleep next to me," Misty said. "Truth be told, I'm kind of scared. Come lie down next to me." I lay down and she placed herself close to me. As tempted as I was to close finally my eyes, I knew I couldn't. Misty looked more than tired, more than scared. The day before, she had been tied to a tree for many hours. She had very little to eat for two days. She wasn't sick exactly, but she looked ill. There was darkness under her eyes. Usually, her sweet brown skin had a healthy glow to it. Now she had a gray cast that concerned me. I wanted to stay there for her and I wanted to sleep because I was tired, too. I couldn't. Tugging at me were the very real responsibilities that only I could fulfill. Everyone, not just Misty, was depending on me to do my best for them. I had to tell Caleb what I read about the guns. We had to be prepared and that had to begin with me. I was the only one who had read the booklet and I was the only one who could tell what I learned from it. I lay there with my eyes wide open for a few minutes, unable to think of anything else. I hoped Misty had fallen asleep when I got back on my feet. "What are you doing?" Misty said, annoyed.

"I have to talk to Caleb," I said.

"Now? Does it have to be right now?"

"I'm sorry. This is important for everyone's safety."

"You'll see him in the morning. Come back and lie down. It can wait."

I knew it couldn't. "I have to. I'll just be a few minutes." That was kind of a lie. I didn't know how much time. It would take as long as it took, and I wasn't going to cut my conversation with Caleb short for Misty. "Just go to sleep. I'll be back." She grumbled and turned over.

It was getting dark quickly, but still it was warmer than usual for November. We had decided there would be no fires to attract unwanted attention. I found Caleb on the other side of the camp, lying on his back, peering into the rapidly changing sky. He looked almost as tired as Misty. I tapped his boot with mine. It startled him and he looked up at me. "I read the instructions for the pistols and you're not going to believe it."

"Keep your voice down," he said. "How many guns are there?"

I crouched down next to him. "Six."

"That's not enough. If they come with a big posse, we're going to be slaughtered."

"Maybe and maybe not. These aren't ordinary guns."

"I don't care how shiny and new they are. Even if every shot counted, after firing our six shots, a decent sized force will overwhelm us before we can reload."

"That's what I'm trying to tell you. Not these guns. They're not like regular guns. Let me explain. Each gun can fire five shots in a row without reloading."

Caleb perked up, but still looked disbelieving. "Five in a row? One right after the other?" I nodded. "You're sure about this?"

"They call it a repeating revolver."

"It's not possible. How can you shoot five times without reloading?"

"The gun has something called a five-chamber cylinder that comes right out of the middle. You take the cylinder and load all five chambers at once, put the gun back together and you're ready to fire off five shots."

He smiled. "That's different alright."

"And I have an idea." I hesitated a little.

"What's your idea? It's okay, tell me."

"We could assign a team to each gun. Each team would have three people, a shooter and two loaders. We can use our best shooters to do nothing but make every one of those fives shots count. Then, two people work to reload, one organizing the supplies, the other loading the cylinder. That way reloading can happen even faster and the pistol will be back in the shooters hand."

"And the single shot posse won't know what hit them by the time they reload after taking their first shot," Caleb said. "Is it hard to learn?"

"No. You pour a charge of powder in the chamber, tap in a ball, then a piece of felt and a cap on the other side. Put the gun back together and you're ready. If you've loaded a single shot gun before, I don't think it's too different, except you're loading five shots all at once."

"Book, I got to say, you being able to read those instructions, well, it's half the fight. Thank you."

"I told you you'd need me to read on this trip. Ha ha." I was pleased. "There's something else. Each pistol came with a spare cylinder. That means the spare can be loaded while the shooter is firing from the first cylinder. Reloading only takes as long as removing the empty cylinder, and replacing it with a fully loaded cylinder. One good shooter with one of these guns is better than any five Light-horse men with old single shot guns."

"Why did Grady's have them?" Caleb said.

"Each gun was packed in a fancy wood box with all the extra equipment. I think they were meant as gifts for the members Council or somebody else important, not really for sale. Lucky for us they never made it out of Grady's. That is, until Cotton Hand got them." We laughed.

"How ever they got to Grady's, I'm grateful they were there when we needed them," Caleb said. "Book, why don't you go lie down and get some sleep. In the morning, we'll put the gun teams together and show them how to load the pistols. You go ahead, now, son. Go lie down. Good work."

I started making my way through the camp to get back to Misty, when Millie jumped in front of me, blocking the way. I was happy to see her. "Millie, I'm glad you're with us. I was afraid you wouldn't be able to get free of that tree."

"Ha! No tree can hold Millie for long." She laughed. "Tall Bone cut me loose before he left. He's a nice man."

"Yes, he is," I agreed.

"Lookie Bookie, I got some food for you. You fed me, now I feed you."

"Lookie Bookie?"

Millie giggled. "Why not? Here, eat some of this. Then you can go on your way to frilly Miss Misty over there. I know that's where you want to go." Her smile disappeared. I felt sorry for her. She was trying hard to be nice to me.

"Come with me, Millie. You can sleep next to us."

"Oh, I don't think Misty would like that at all."

"It's alright."

"I better not. I don't want to start another fight." She looked me in the eyes. "But you are a sweet one, aren't you? I knew that all along." She lightly touched my nose with her finger. "See you in the morning, sweetie."

When I first met Millie, I mistrusted her. I also misjudged her. Without wanting to be, she had been thrown into the middle of a serious situation between Missus and me. Following Missus's orders, she had almost no choice in what she did, which gave the appearance that she was betraying her fellow slaves. What she reported to Missus, though, at her own risk, actually protected Misty and me as much as she could. At the time, I was so sensitive to every, little thing, I even mistook her flirting and playfulness for a threat. In her own way, she stood up to Missus and that took great strength and a good heart. And she did it with charm and humor, just what I was lacking. A lot of what she was, I was not, but wanted to be. Where my thoughts had been scattered and frantic, she was calculating and smooth. Where I was constantly worried about the worst happening, she was ready for the worst but saw the bright side. I had to admit that I was wrong about Millie. I wouldn't make that mistake again.

I lay down on the blanket that Misty had spread for us. Our first day as runaways was long and difficult, and she was already asleep, breathing heavily. It almost sounded like sighing. The moonlight illuminated her lovely profile. I could have stared at her for hours, but my exhaustion overcame me and I slept. My sleep was not peaceful. I kept dreaming different versions of the same dream, over and over. In my dream, Bandana was noisily nickering while pounding the ground with her front left hoof, all to get my attention. She led me into dark woods. A young woman stood beside me, but I couldn't see her face clearly. There was danger, possibly even death behind me. Bandana kept beckoning me further and deeper into the woods. I was lost, leaving behind all that was familiar. Eventually the sounds of danger could no longer be heard. I was confused, but trusted Bandana.

I awoke at daybreak to see a prairie chicken casually pecking at scraps from last night's meal. I thought, if I had a little more spunk, that prairie chicken might become part of that night's supper. Instead, I just lay there when suddenly a hand reached down and grabbed the bird. It was Millie's hand. She was awake and strong and ready for the day's challenges. "Nice catch," I said sleepily.

She called out, "You bet. I never let a good chicken get by me. But I see that you do, sleepyhead. Ha ha," she joked as she took the struggling bird over to Rose to show off her catch.

Before I was fully awake, Caleb pulled me up by the arm and guided me to the wagon where he had already chosen and grouped the three-person loading, shooting teams. "This is Book Boy," he announced to the six teams. "As some of you already know, Book Boy is our reader. He's smart and he can read anything. He read this book about using the new guns." He held up the instruction booklet. "These are very different from any guns I've ever seen. Different and better. Listen to him carefully. The better you learn your part in using these guns, the better our chances to get to Mexico alive." He put his arm around me and handed me the booklet. "Okay, Book. Tell us what to do. But don't take too long because I got the feeling we're going to be shooting these guns mighty soon." Caleb joined one of the groups as they all seated themselves on the ground in a half circle in front of me. I looked at their faces, set on learning how they would survive what we all believed would be a fight to the death. It was early in the day, but already getting warm. It felt more like May or June 18th, not November 18th. I squinted in the sunshine and began my talk.

"I only know what the book says. I have never fired this or any other gun." The group groaned.

One of the men stood up. "Then what do you know? At least I shot a gun. Let me see one of those things, I'll tell you how it works." He started walking toward me and the boxes of guns next to me when Caleb put himself in the way.

"You best go and sit down and listen. Go on," Caleb said to me. The man returned to his place but didn't sit down.

"I didn't come all this way to risk my neck to have some fool boy who never shot anything tell me how to shoot. Just give me my gun and I'll be going," the man said.

"Look. I don't know you." Caleb said. "You're not from the Vanner place, are you?"

"No, I'm not. Does that matter?"

"It hasn't mattered until right now," Caleb said. "How did you come to be with us?"

"I'm from another plantation owned by the Vanner family. There are a few of us here. We want out as much as you do, but I won't be taking orders from a kid."

"You will take orders from me and I'm telling you to learn from this kid. His name is Book Boy because he can read. Books. You know what books are?"

"Sure I know what books are."

"Can you read them?"

"You know I can't. Can you?"

"No, I can't. But he can. And he read the book on how to use this new gun. In point of fact, he's the only one who knows how. So shut up and listen or you won't get in ten feet of these guns. Understand?" Caleb glared at him menacingly and the man, mumbling to himself, sat back down. "Go ahead, Book."

"This is a new kind of gun. Nobody here has ever fired one like this." I held up one of the spare cylinders. "It has a cylinder with five chambers. You can load a ball and a cap in each chamber. That means that just one of these guns can fire five shots in a row without having to reload." They looked at me in disbelief.

"How does it do that?" one of them asked.

"When you fire one ball, the cylinder that holds the ammunition clicks another loaded chamber into place, ready to fire the next ball. They call it a revolver." They were starting to understand. "Alright. Each team come and get one of these boxes, but don't do anything until I tell you. Also, we are not going to fire them until we are shooting at the enemy. We have no ammunition to waste. So, we're going to learn is how to load fast, but no shooting practice. That alright with you, Caleb?"

"Sounds right to me, Book." Caleb stood and faced the group. "No shooting until you're shooting at the enemy, and no shooting at the enemy until I give you the word." He waved his arm. "Go on, Book. You're doing fine." Caleb winked at me.

We spent the next half hour making sure everyone knew how to load and shoot the guns. When we were done, every cylinder was loaded, even the spares, and every gun assembled. We were ready for war. It was time to start our day's ride. Many of them came to thank me for the lesson, patting me on the back as they left. Millie was one of the one's who came up to me, but she didn't pat me on the back, exactly.

"You were good, Mr. Bookie. Real good." Then she giggled and slapped my hind end, which made me jump up in the air. Everyone who saw, including Caleb, laughed.

"Watch out for that one, Book," he said with a smile.

"I guess I should, shouldn't I?" I said, still bewildered by Millie's forthright ways.

CHAPTER 8

We had crossed Dirty Creek and traveled far beyond the narrow band of trees that lined it. I never felt so isolated and small. Even though I was surrounded by over twenty fellow souls, all of us escaping southward toward Mexico, in every direction the countryside was still and silent. The pale, brown grass waving in the slight breeze, provided the only movement, with hardly a tree to break the straight line of the flat horizon. All the while, the nagging thought that we were being tracked by a well-armed posse weighed heavily on my mind. Where were they? How close? Why hadn't they found us yet? I almost wished they would finally find us to get the battle over with. I had never been in a fist-fight before, much less a battle with shooting. Mr. Money Joe had a book about famous wars and their generals, and I had read about Alexander the Great, Julius Caesar, Napoleon, even General George Washington. I didn't understand some of the words, but something that stuck with me was that most of the generals were sure that they would eventually win. They fought without any fear of death, as if there was no chance they could be defeated. They weren't afraid of losing as many their soldiers as it took, either. All except General Washington. He wasn't like the other generals. Washington counted and re-counted his men, as though each one was precious. If it looked like he might lose a battle, he would rather sneak away from the enemy before it started. If he was running, he would save his army to fight another day. He would only fight a battle he thought he could win. It worked, too. It took a long time, but he won in the end. That's what we should do, I thought. If Napoleon got his men killed, he could always put together another army. But not us. We were all we had. Each one of us was important, precious, like Washington's soldiers. We needed each other to survive out here, in the lonely wilderness.

Another day went by. Maybe two. I'm not sure how many, as each seemed just like the one before it. Off the main trail, it was slow going as we rode through the open stretch of flat, brown land, mostly in tired silence, as though too much talk might attract attention. No one was there to listen. There was no sign of the angry, vengeful posse I had imagined. I assumed that Mr. Money Joe would be so furious about the loss of this many of his most valuable slaves that he would immediately finance an army of Light-horse men to track us down and drag us back in chains. No such army appeared. Jumping Ben, riding at the head of our column with Caleb, had been leading us steadily south. Somehow, Ben found us water, warning that the waterholes would become fewer as we got closer to Texas, and so would the grass that fed the horses which sprouted around the water. Our food stock was gradually disappearing, and hunting meant venturing into the woods away from the others, using valuable ammunition that would be needed for our defense. We kept putting off hunting for food and, in the main, relying on what we had packed in the wagon and our saddlebags. Of course, as Millie had discovered, a lost prairie chicken might help us out by unknowingly wandering into our hungry camp.

On and off since we began, thunder could be heard. We saw no rain. We only heard the drumming far away. Occasionally, a loud, isolated boom would startle me, making me think an attack had begun. I sensed that there was bad weather in motion out there and it was bound to meet up with us soon. So far, though, we had warm, sunny days, helping me to become a better rider. Marigold and I were getting along fine. Most days, I would ride next to Misty. On this particular day, she wasn't feeling well enough to ride, so she sat next to Rose in the wagon. I trotted Marigold up to the front, to ride with Caleb and Ben for a while. They were discussing what we might expect to happen next. Just as I came within earshot of something Ben said about the Canadian River, there was some sort of commotion in the rear of our column. I heard Rose and Misty shouting, "Caleb! Bone! Cotton! Book! Come over here, quick. Fast! We need you here now!" Caleb turned his horse right around and sped back to the wagon. I followed the best I could. When I got there Caleb, Bone and Cotton had already fixed their gaze on something in the distance. Rose and Misty were pointing to the western horizon.

As I pulled up near the wagon, Misty shouted, "Book! Look over there, Book. Those people are walking straight to us. You think it's them? The posse? Should we pass out the guns?"

Caleb said, "Whoa, hold on. Now, why would a posse be on foot? The only people on foot in this big, open, nowhere country are people with no horses. Those are slaves. I think so anyway. Keep the guns in the wagon till we see what's up."

As they approached, I could make them out more clearly. "They look kind of dark-skinned. I think they're African, like us. One of them is limping." As I spoke, the limping man fell to the ground. "Should we go help them, Caleb?"

Tall Bone and his big heart answered for him. "Of course we should. They must be runaways, too."

Cotton cautioned, "We don't know who they are. Maybe they're slaves. Maybe they used to be slaves, and now they're a runaway gang looking to rob and murder. We've got to be careful. I see about ten of them."

Tall Bone agreed. "You're right Cotton. We just don't know. We have about fifteen or twenty minutes until they get here. I say we break out the guns and keep them handy if we need them. I think we should keep the guns on us all the time from now on. What good do they do locked up in the wagon if there's trouble?"

"I think he's right, Caleb. No shooting unless there's trouble, but we need to be ready. The shooters should have their guns on them," I said.

Caleb thought for a minute. His mouth curled down into a thoughtful frown. "Alright. Hand out the guns, Book. Make sure everybody knows they are just for an emergency. We have no ammunition to waste, and we don't want to start any unnecessary trouble. They only shoot if they see me shoot."

I climbed into the wagon and began opening the boxes, removing the loaded guns. Misty squatted down next to me. "How do you feel?" I asked her.

"Scared."

"I think they're just runaways, like us," I said.

"It's the guns. They're so dangerous. I don't even want to look at them. I know what they can do."

There was something in Misty's past that she had never told me. Something bad. I wanted to know what it was. "What did you see, Misty?" I asked as I lined up the guns.

"It's not what I saw, exactly," she whispered. She had a cold, distant look in her eyes. This was different for Misty. I had seen her scared before. This had more to do with her than what she saw someone else do. "It's what I did. What I had to do." This was not the time for stories from the past, but if she needed to tell me, I would listen.

"Misty, can you tell me while I'm doing this?" I had placed the guns in a canvas bag to carry them to the shooters.

"No. I'm fine." She touched my face. "Book, I'm alright." Her thoughts returned to our situation. "I think they are runaways. What if they want to join us! We hardly have enough for ourselves." I was taken aback by her lack of sympathy, but I could understand it. Each day we watched our food disappearing. We slept little, and were tired and frightened all the time, constantly looking over our shoulders for signs of a posse we knew would come. Still, how could we turn our backs on these poor souls, if they were who we thought they were?

"I have to hand out these guns. Everything will be fine," I told her. I scrambled out of the wagon, my sack in hand and one by one, found those who had been designated as the shooters. I gave them Caleb's instructions to keep the weapons ready, but only to shoot when and if they saw him shoot. When I was finished, I mounted my horse and joined Caleb, Tall Bone, Cotton Hand and Jumping Ben, who were facing the men walking toward us. We slowly rode out to confront them, before they were in the midst of our people, just in case they meant trouble.

Caleb shouted out to them in the field. "Hey you. Hey. What do you want? Who are you?" The men kept walking toward us. Caleb held up his pistol. "Stop right there. That's far enough." They stopped. "Who are you? Where are you from?"

One of them answered, "Sir, we are slaves who ran away from our Creek master. We want to be free, same as you."

Caleb lowered his gun. "How long have you been running?"

"I think a few days, sir. I'm not sure. We have had no food or water for a while and..." With that he fell to his knees and then collapsed onto the ground, unable to move. His companions rushed to him.

Caleb and I got off our horses and went to him. He was still alive, but just barely. That could have been said of them all. Their mouths were cracked and dry. Their clothes were ragged and filthy. That was it. We had no fight on our hands, but a rescue. Ben found a nearby place for us to make camp. They had been lost and wandering, dying of thirst, with water just a short distance away. Our numbers had suddenly grown by ten more runaway slaves from the Creek Nation.

As we sat and ate with them we learned their story from a young man not much older than I was. "We all worked on the same farm, but the summer was hot and dry, so there wasn't much of a harvest. Every day without rain the master got a little crazier, talking a little more nonsense. He started beating us for no reason, blaming us for the bad weather and poor crops. He said we were doing some kind of magic against him. His overseer complained about not being paid and quit. Then the master started beating his wife, too, saying that she had, you know, been with the overseer. She left him. I don't know where she went, but she was gone for good. Then it was just us and the crazy master. I guess he owed a lot of money, because he decided to sell everything, including us. With him pointing a gun at us, we were walking on the road, I guess to where they sell slaves. I thought, if we can get that gun from him, we could escape. After all, there were ten of us and just one of him. That gun was the only thing between us and freedom. I pretended to trip and twist my ankle. He cursed me, waving his musket and shouting for me to get up. I pulled on the musket with all my strength and he fell. The musket just seemed to go off. He sat there, eyes open, looking at me, a ball through his chest, dead. We started running. Didn't know where we were going or how to get there. Just running. Left his horse. Left his musket."

"So he was dead? You killed him?" I asked.

"Left him dead, face down on the ground."

"What did you do after...you know?" I asked.

"Like I said, we just ran right out of that place. We stole food from a couple of houses. That was gone fast. Then we just wandered around looking for food, a place to hide, getting nowhere."

"Did anyone come looking for you?" Tall Bone asked.

"I don't know. There was nobody around. I don't expect anybody would miss the bad man. When they do find him face down, I suppose they'll figure out what happened and come looking for us." He grinned, "I swear, it's just a miracle, a miracle, I say, that we were fortunate enough to met up with you all. I swear, we'd have been face down dead ourselves before long. Yes, sir, a miracle."

After hearing the story, Bone and I looked at each other. We both knew that the Creeks would never rest in the hunt for these slaves. They weren't simply runaways. They had murdered their master. The Creeks would never let go of a crime like that, no matter how bad a man that master was. And if the master owed a substantial amount of money, the people who held his debts would also want the slaves found, to be sold off and used as payment. They might even finance the cost of a posse to catch the runaways. Bone leaned over and whispered to me, "They are coming to find these boys, you better believe it. And they are coming hard on the trail. Bound to be out there right now, following their crooked path that hardly took them anywhere. That posse won't have far to go from home to right here. Just a matter of time till they get to us. I wonder whose posse will get here first, theirs or ours?" I didn't laugh.

"Bone," I said quietly. "Are we making a mistake taking them with us?"

"Most likely, yes," Bone said, gesturing toward the stranger. He had gone back to eating, appearing not to pay us any mind, but I thought by his alert posture that he was listening all the same.

"But how can we just put them back out there? That's us, too. We're runaways, out there, too. We can't say no. Maybe it'll work out for the best in the end."

I was unconvinced, and so were many of the others. From the first, we had accepted that we were being hunted and that we could be attacked at any time. Yet having these men traveling with us, as part of our group, put us even more at risk, even more on edge, if that was possible. There was plenty of resentment among our people. Some, not even considering the posse that I was certain was hurrying on its way, openly worried that with more mouths to feed, we would run out of supplies that much faster. Caleb's leadership was called into question. A committee of four or five people approached him, saying that they thought feeding the strangers was good enough and in the morning we should part ways with them.

"Caleb, think about it," said one of them, a man who I recognized as a field worker. He had a reputation for his strength and I had seen him doing heavy work other men couldn't do. "By my count, there's ten of them. Ten hungry men with no horses. Now, what do you think that will do for us? Will it make us faster? No. Safer? No. Everybody knows that having them travel with us is going to slow us down and eat up our supplies. It will take forever to get to Mexico with them on foot. I risked my life to seal up the overseer's house so we could slow Mr. Money Joe down. It was risky, but a good idea and I was glad to do it. And now, by taking them in, taking away that edge I gained us, any advantage we had by getting a head start on Money Joe's men will be lost. So why did I risk my life?" His friends all showed their approval for what he was saying. Seeing this, he started using the word 'we', speaking for all of them. "We say, come morning, they have to go. That's what we want."

Caleb was afraid that his decision to let the strangers join us might lead to splitting our original group into fragments, with some of the group wanting to set out on their own. Such a division would undoubtedly weaken our ability to fight, to survive. There would be time wasted quarreling about dividing the guns, the food, the ammunition, the horses, the wagon. We would become our own enemies, possibly fight amongst ourselves for the limited supplies. Caleb's generous heart was telling him to find a way of satisfying this committee without completely abandoning the strangers who he saw as brother slaves, not freeloaders. "Ben," he called. "Could you come here, please?" Ben reluctantly walked over to join the conversation. He hesitated to become involved in the leadership decisions, his role being strictly a guide who was with us temporarily. "Ben, how long, do you suppose, before we get to the Canadian River crossing?" Caleb turned to the committee. "That's the big river we'll soon have to cross to keep heading south," he explained.

Ben was relieved that it was just a guide question. He put his hand to chin thoughtfully. Then he peered deeply into the dusky horizon as though he could see what none of us could see. "I'd say... one more full day's ride and we'll be there. But, with them on foot, maybe more like two days. That's just to reach the river. We want to find a particular part of the river, the place where there's an island in the middle to make it much safer for us to cross. When we get closer, I'll ride ahead and find the island. I'll know more then, but I'm thinking it will be near the end of two days from now."

"Thanks, Ben. I think I know what we should do. Tell me if this sounds good to you?" Caleb said, meeting the eyes of the committee leader. "The strangers stay with us only until we cross the river. Once we're all on the other side of the river, they go their way, and we go our way. Let the river be the mark when they leave us. Their trail will end at the water's edge and that will at least give them a chance to lose anyone following them. Fair enough?"

The committee man shook his head no. "Too much bad can happen in two days. I still don't like it." He thought for a moment and said, "What if they follow us in back of the wagon, and do what they can to keep pace. That way they don't slow us down too much, and they catch up when we stop to make camp. Also, they don't get guns and all the food stays with us."

Caleb was pleased. "That's a good plan," Caleb said as he thrust out his hand and firmly shook. The man was also pleased that he had gotten some concessions from Caleb. The rest of the committee slapped his back and I could tell from his face that he felt very important. I actually agreed with him at the time. I didn't have the same feeling of kinship that Caleb had with other slaves. The limited supplies were certainly a worry, but more important to me was the fact that it was our original group who had worked so hard to conceive and carry out the plan of escape, not these strangers who now wanted only to benefit from our work without having earned it for themselves. If it had been left up to me, I would have sent them on their way at daybreak. Before we went to sleep, Misty and I talked about it. "It's not that I don't understand why they killed their master," I told her. "But was it truly necessary that he die for them to escape? Look at us. We chose a different way to leave. We killed no one. Cotton Hand was always going on about how he wants to kill this one and that one. He didn't do it. He left hurting nobody."

Misty was a little more sympathetic toward them. "According to them he was a bad man who beat them. Maybe he had it coming."

"So they killed him as a punishment? Don't misunderstand. I would kill anyone who threatened us or tried to prevent our escape. I'm no fool. It's just that he said the musket seemed to go off after the master had fallen to the ground and was sitting there, looking at him. After. Then the trigger pulled itself?"

"I don't have any pity for any slave owner. Especially one who treats his slaves so badly," she said.

"I suppose you're right. It's going to bring a posse down on them, though. I'm certain of that. I hope we get rid of them before that happens."

She snuggled into me. "So far, everything is good. Let's get some sleep."

She kissed me and fell asleep right away. I lay awake for a while, worrying about the doom I saw coming. I could feel it. I just couldn't name it or say when it would arrive. The horses knew, too. They couldn't make themselves comfortable, either.

That night, Misty slept with my arm curled around her in some way, whether she slept on her back, her left side or her right side. I felt uneasy, like something very bad was about to happen. Part of it was that I didn't trust the strangers. Why would I? I hardly knew anything about them, except that they were killers. In the morning, we awoke to the sound of thunder. This time, it wasn't very far away. Then rain came, in big, heavy drops. A few at first. The ones that landed on my skin stung. I realized that it wasn't ordinary rain. This rain was hard and solid when it fell from the sky. They were round pieces of ice and they were getting bigger and heavier. Misty cried out as they struck us. The hail began piling up on our blankets and our supplies. It pelted the horses, making them angry and confused. They bucked and whinnied. Ben called them hailstones and told us it wasn't safe for the horses to be tied to anything. He said they would find us when the storm was over, so we let them run off. I was hoping he was right about them coming back. The wind was getting stronger, adding to the speed of the hail hitting us. We put the blankets over our heads. They soon became heavy with hail. Misty and I looked up at the sky from under our blanket. I had never seen anything like it. There was a dense, dark, almost black cloud stretching across the sky except for one part.

"Misty. Look over there. The sky over there is green." It was a strange and frightening thing to see. I called out to Ben, pointing to the sky. "Ben! Look over there. The sky is green."

Ben shouted, "The unole is coming. Everyone, stay away from the wagon. Stay away from trees. Find some low ground and lie down flat. Pray the unole passes by without touching you!"

The hail turned to driving rain that pounded my back as the ferocious wind gusted. Small objects were easily scattered at random. Our blanket filled with wind, billowing and nearly lifting us off the ground. There was no way that we could safely hold onto it. We let go and the blanket was immediately airborne. We didn't wait to see where it landed. Misty and I voluntarily dropped down, flat on the ground, to keep the wind from forcing us to fall over. As I lay there, I saw the storm. It was like a hideous, giant finger, extending down from the black cloud above, tearing at the earth. Whatever the finger touched was flung about. It was impossible to predict where the finger would go next, but it was coming closer to us. As it did, I could see that it was a cloud of swirling dust and debris, constantly spinning and moving erratically. One minute this way, next minute the opposite direction. I put my body on top of Misty to protect her. The spinning finger had so much power, I was sure it could easily pull us up from the ground and throw us into the air. I had nothing to hold on to. As the finger approached us the roar of the wind was so loud, it drowned out the screams of the frightened people. Misty covered her face, praying for it to be over. I couldn't help raising my head to look. It was terrifying but fascinating. I remember seeing a rock lifted by the wind and thrown directly toward my head, then... nothing.

When I opened my eyes, I was flat on my back looking up, a girl's face hovered over me. She gently dusted debris from my hair and face. I recall enjoying the comforting feel of her healing hand on my forehead. Her touch was unafraid and honest, yet sweet and warm.

I had trouble forming words, at first. "Is...is...that you? Mi....Mi...?"

"Better get the rest of that name right, Bookie Boy," she laughed.

"Millie?" I said. Somehow, I wasn't really surprised that it was Millie tending to me. I started laughing with her, relieved that I was alive enough to laugh.

"That's the name, alright. And don't you forget it," she said. Tenderly, she said, "Don't worry. You'll be fine, my dear. Just a bump on that hard head of yours."

"Is everyone else alright? Anyone hurt?"

"A few cuts and bruises. You got the worst of it, I think. Knocked out, cold."

I suddenly noticed how quiet it was. The sky was actually blue and peaceful. The angry green and black was gone. People were busy, collecting their things, preparing to resume our journey. "Have I been asleep a long time, Millie?"

"No, not too long. Maybe a half hour. A couple of minutes after you were hit, the storm was over."

"You saw me hit?"

Millie hesitated. She looked a little embarrassed. "I guess I was watching you," she whispered. I wanted to pull her toward me and hug her. Then I remembered my situation.

"Uh. Where's Misty?"

"Oh. I saw her go over there. She's in the wagon with Rose. She was kind of shaken up by the storm. When we get going, she'll be riding there today." Millie took my face in her hands. "You look pretty good to me, young man. You feel strong enough to ride your horse, now?"

I did have a slight headache and I could feel a lump where the rock hit me, but I felt well enough to ride. "I think so." I put my hands over her hands, which were still on my face. "Thank you, Millie. Thank you for everything." With her steady hands calming me, I felt more than just gratitude.

She pulled her hands away slowly. "Oh, it's nothing," she said softly. "Better tell Caleb you're ready to get moving, Bookie." Millie was the only person who had ever called me 'Bookie'. It was getting to be a habit for her, and I enjoyed having something special between us.

I wanted to stay near her shining smile and the warmth of her personality. "Maybe you could ride with me today, I mean in case I get too dizzy or something?" As I said the words, I knew they didn't make any sense. It was easy to guess that I was making up a reason for us to be together.

I'm sure Millie understood perfectly, but she played right along. "Well, if you think it would be a good idea, I'd be glad to keep an eye on you, Bookie." There was a real happiness in her eyes, the kind that comes from being appreciated by someone you care about. Millie knew, even before I did, how much I genuinely liked her. I got on my horse and turned myself around to see the wagon. I waved my arm to let Misty know I was okay, but she didn't see me. It was Rose who waved back. She pointed to me, saying something I couldn't hear to Misty. Misty didn't respond, only looking straight ahead. I couldn't tell if she was angry or still in shock from the storm. It had been a terrifying experience for both of us, for all of us.

We were running dangerously low on food and water. My stomach was growling, as I'm sure everybody's was, but no one ate. Without saying a word about it, we all knew that we had to stretch whatever was left as long as we possibly could. I offered Millie some water from a pouch that hung on my saddle.

"No thanks. You have it," she said. I put it away. "How long do you think before we get to the river? This isn't the Texas river, right."

"No, it's not the Red River. This is the Canadian. I guess we'll see woods in the distance just before we get to it. Trees grow near the water."

"Hey. If there are woods, there would be animals."

"I reckon so."

"Animals we could eat?"

"That may be. I could go for a nice, fat…" My sentence was cut off by the sight of trees on the horizon. I was surprised that my prediction had come true so quickly. "Look straight ahead. Those are trees, aren't they?" The flat brown grass would come to an end after all.

"I just love trees," Millie said cheerfully. "Don't you?" We laughed. I overheard Ben telling Caleb he would ride ahead to look for the crossing. Caleb waived his arm for me to come to him at the front of our column.

"Caleb wants me, Millie. I'll see you later."

"See you 'round, Bookie," she said and winked at me.

Caleb and Ben were waiting for me. "How are you feeling, Book?" Ben asked me. "I see you got a nice bump there in the storm."

"I'm okay. I was really out for a while."

"We're coming to the river soon," Caleb said. "Ben is going to ride ahead to look for the crossing. I don't want him to go alone. I want you to go with him. Do you think you're up to it?"

"Sure, I'll go. I think my horse could use some grass and water, though. She's kind of slowing down."

"Everybody's horse is slowing down, but we've still got to keep moving," Caleb said. "Here, take this." He held out his gun.

I was shocked. "Are you sure?"

"Yes, I'm sure. You should to be able to back up Ben if something happens."

I took the gun. "This thing is heavy, isn't it? Where do I put it?"

Caleb chuckled. "Stick it in your jeans. Be careful you don't shoot yourself, son." As uncomfortable as I was, I did as I was told. I trusted Ben to know what he was doing, because I surely did not. Ben and I rode off, armed and ready, though for what I didn't know.

Without the wagon and the strangers on foot to slow us down, Ben and I rode swiftly toward the trees. The leaves had recently changed color from green to brilliant yellow and red-orange. Against the pure, cloudless blue sky, the colors of the day were magnificent. As we rode along the edge of the woods, I was feeling better and stronger about being on this surprise mission. The gun in my waistband was both frightening and reassuring. I wondered if I would be able to shoot if it became necessary. I knew how the gun worked alright, having studied the instruction booklet well enough to teach the others. But knowing how from a book and pointing the gun at another person are two very different things. Back in Webb's Bend, I had nothing to do with guns, not even for hunting. I may as well have been a city boy for all my lack of firearm experience. At least Ben was a hunter, one of the best. He and Annie practically lived off of his hunting skill. I wondered how she was getting along without him.

"It should be a few more miles up this way," Ben said. We can cut into the woods up there and..." He was interrupted by the distant sound of screams coming from the woods.

We stopped to listen. "Is that coming from up ahead?" I asked. "I don't think it's from our camp."

Ben agreed. "You're right, it's that way. Let's have a look." He took off at a gallop. Before I knew it my horse was galloping too, following Ben's. I was lucky to be holding on, being swept to who-knows-where by my horse. The screams were getting louder. I could make out several separate voices, a man, a woman, children. What could they possibly be doing in this wilderness? The answer came quickly. The screams were from a group of people, huddled together. They appeared to be a family, a man, a woman, three children of various young ages. Their ragged, homemade clothes and African skin told me they were slaves. They were cringing from a mountain lion, peering at them menacingly, from a tree limb, ready to pounce on them, ready to tear them to pieces. They couldn't do much about it except scream, because the adults' hands were tied and their feet were shackled with chains. The children clung to their parents with terror in their eyes. The man's gaze kept shifting from the big cat to something behind some trees that, at first, I couldn't make out.

"Ben, what's he looking at behind those trees?"

"I don't know, let's get in closer." As we did, we saw two white men on horseback laughing at the frightened family. "You have your five-shot revolver handy?" he said quietly.

I pulled it out. "Yes," I answered, just as quietly.

"Fire a single shot in the air to scare off the animal." I cocked the gun, pointed it to the blue sky and pulled the trigger. The loud bang startled the mountain lion and sent him running away. It startled me, too. The noise also called attention to Ben and me. We had, until that moment, remained unnoticed by the two men. They abruptly stopped laughing at the sound of the gunshot and turned to face the direction the sound had come from, which was me. The men had been passing a flask back and forth between them, taking long gulps between laughing at the plight of the family. I later understood that the strange, sickly smell they carried was from drinking whiskey, a lot of it, every day. Strong drink was illegal in the Indian territory, except for whites, but it could be had. Missus never allowed any alcoholic beverage at the Vanner place so I had no first hand knowledge about it, only what I'd read here and there. Even with my lack of experience, it was plain to me that these two were drunk.

"Well, well. what's this?" the bearded one said. He looked at Ben, who was cradling his musket. The man's mouth slowly curled up into a cruel smile. "We don't want trouble, here, my brother. We're just a couple of honest, lawful slave catchers plying our trade. We don't want to hurt nobody." He pointed to the family. "They ran away and we caught 'em. That's the long and the short of it." He laughed and took the flask from the other slave catcher. "Can I offer you a pull on the bottle, my brother?" He held out the flask in Ben's direction. Ben waved him off. "We're just on our way to bring them back to their Creek master." As he looked at us, he noticed that it was me, not Ben, who fired the shot that scared off the mountain lion, because I was still holding my gun, pointing it to the sky. I could see him puzzling over this. "Can I ask you, since when do my Creek brothers let their slaves carry guns?"

Calmly and clearly Ben said, "I am not Creek. Also, I am not your brother. And he is not a slave."

"Well then, in that case, you best stop right there," the man bellowed as he quickly drew his pistol and trained it on Ben. "No, you're not a Creek, are you?" He looked puzzled. "If you're no Creek and you're no slave, then what are you two?"

The other man spoke up in a slow drawl. "Wait a minute, Ruggs," he said, referring to the bearded man. "I know. I know." He wagged his finger at Ben. "I'll bet he's that Cherokee we heard about in town. Yes sir. He's the one who helped all them slaves run away. That you, mister?" He looked at Ben for a reaction. When Ben didn't deny what the slaver had said, the man grinned, delighted with himself for having figured out who we were. "It is you! Ha! That's it! Ha! That's it! And he," nodding toward me, "must be one of the them runaway slaves."

Ruggs appeared happy, too, behind his beard. "Is that what you are, boy? You a runaway slave, boy?" He looked me over. "You're mighty far from home. You miss your home, boy? Don't worry, I'll help you get back. That's what I do. I help homesick slaves get back to their masters. Come on now." He waved his gun. "Get down off that horse. You're going home, boy. You too, Mister Cherokee. You're both going home."

"Hey, if it is the Cherokee, then there's a whole lot more of him nearby," the other one said of me. "This could be big money, Ruggs." He was so excited, he let go with a long, loud yell. "OOOOWEEE! Big money!"

Rugg's smile faded fast and his gazed turned steely serious. "You boys must be worth a fortune to the right person." he said.

I held my arm straight out, pointing my gun square at his chest. This horrible man meant to take me, take Misty, take Millie, take Caleb, take all of us, back to slavery and turn Ben over to the Light-horse. I could not let that happen. I would not let that happen. The mechanical sound of me cocking my gun brought a derisive laugh from the two slave catchers.

"Boy, you are one ignorant slave." He looked at his partner, grinning. "Let me spell this out for you, slave. You already spent your shot, boy. And I was watching you the whole time, so I know you didn't re-load. The only way you could hurt me with that gun now is to throw it at me. It might as well be a rock or something. Like the one you got for a head." Again he looked over to his partner who laughed hysterically. "With brains like that you're way better off back on the farm as a slave. You wouldn't last a day on your own, out in the real world." He held out his hand. "Time to get off the horse, boy, and give me that gun, or you just might make me mad, in which instance I will have to blow your head clean off your shoulders, reward or no reward. You understanding me, rock head?" The gun, which he had pointed at Ben, he now swung over to threaten me. Suddenly, I heard the sharp crack of another shot fired. I saw the astounded look on the bearded man's, face as his body crumpled and then slid, limply off of his horse. It was my gun that fired. I had killed him. There he was, blood gushing from the hole in his chest, forming a muddy red pool in the dirt. I looked up and pointed the weapon at the second man. Shocked, he took off at a gallop. I fired at him. This time I missed. Ben held up his hand for me to stop. He placed his musket in firing position and flipped up the sight on the barrel to help him aim. He steadied his arm as the musket barrel smoothly followed the path of the second slave catcher across the horizon. Even though I knew it was coming, I was still startled by the crack of Ben's musket. A moment later, the slave catcher slumped in his saddle, the horse still galloping off into the distance, the hooves striking the hard ground with an echo, the dead rider somehow still attached to the saddle. Then something must have loosened up and the rider tumbled to the ground, the horse continuing to gallop on his own, growing smaller and smaller as he ran.

As I watched the rider's death from a distance, I began to feel a vague wave of sadness come over me, like a hazy fog, disorienting me, making it difficult to breathe. I have called it the fog of death ever since. I had killed a man. Yes, I had good reason to do it and he was an evil man, capturing and tormenting slaves, but the fact remained, I was responsible for the deliberate death of a person. The fog didn't prevent me from seeing, moving about, talking. It was just there, invisible to others, an invisible sadness. Not guilt, mind you. I didn't feel guilty, as though I should be punished for some wrongdoing. I reminded myself that what Ben and I had done was right and just. Maybe my revulsion came from simply participating in death. I was diminished, less pure. Maybe it was the idea that I had no other choice, that, in this world, as it is, killing had to be done. In a dim corner of me, a corner I try not to look in too often, that sadness still lingers.

I became aware that there were people staring at me, people who were not at all sad about what I had done. They were the family of runaway slaves who Ben and I had just saved. Still in the fog, I got off my horse and searched the dead man's saddlebag, quickly finding the key that would unlock the shackles binding the mother and father. As soon as they were able to move freely, they knelt in front of me, hugging my legs and kissing my hands.

I was embarrassed. "Please. Please stop. Please get up."

"You are a great man," the father said to me with tears in his eyes. He spoke with a foreign accent. I guessed that he had spent most of his life in Africa, but learned to speak English fairly well in the short time he had been in America. "You have saved us with greater courage than the mountain lion. You chased the lion. You killed the evil one. Then you freed us." He held my arms in his hands and looked me in the eye. Slowly, he said, "You are a great man." The woman, though silent, nodded her head in agreement, also with smiling tears. The children were still afraid and ran to their mother, clinging to her and each other. The father's words rang in my head, piercing the fog. That was the first time in my life I had been called a man. I accepted his words. I felt like a man. I hoped that, as a man, my life would not always be so serious and sad as this day had become.

One by one, I lifted the three children onto the dead man's horse. I invited the mother and father to ride my horse, but they politely refused. "It is for you to ride and for us to walk," the father said. I looked over to Ben and saw that he was sad, as well. It was not like him to show so much emotion on his face.

"Ben, what's wrong?"

He fought the tears welling up in his eyes. He wiped them as they came. "Those men knew that I helped you and the other slaves to escape. If they knew, then everyone knows. Even worse, I killed a white man. These are hanging crimes, unforgivable. I can never go back to Webb's Bend." He lowered his voice as if he could not bear to hear the next words to come from his mouth. "Book Boy, I can never go home to my Annie. I will never see her again." He closed his eyes and covered his face with his hands in despair.

The father saw what was happening. He walked over to Ben who was still seated on his horse and reached up to touch Ben's leg. Ben looked down as the father said, "Please do not be unhappy, my brother. Perhaps your Annie can also leave the Webb's Bend and meet you somewhere else where they will not find you. Then you can be together again."

Ben looked down at the father. His face showed some relief. He took a deep breath. "Yes. That is good. She can meet me. I will find a way to get word to her and we will be together." He felt better having a plan for the future. His usual determination and self-confidence returned. "Thank you my brother." Ben turned to me. "I'll continue looking for the crossing. I'm sure it's not too much further. Bring our new friends back to camp and wait for me. Tell Caleb everything that happened today. And tell him we will cross the river tomorrow."

CHAPTER 9

I led the runaway family back to the camp. They were deeply tired and hungry. The children were so thin, I wondered how they were still alive. Their clothes were little more than rags. Missus would have discarded them or had them torn into cleaning cloths long ago. She would never have let me or any of her slaves wear such clothing. I could see there was a great difference between masters, as Missus had warned me when she wanted me to turn over Caleb to the Light-horse men to save her plantation from a new owner, or so she said. It didn't change anything for me, of course. I could never accept being a slave willingly, no matter the temperament of the master. Yet it did justify some of the affection I still couldn't help feeling toward Missus, even though I did my best to swallow hard and forget about her. She had taught me to read and write and cipher numbers and a hundred other things about running a plantation. I still didn't know why she had acted so kindly toward me, or was so interested in my welfare, but I counted myself as lucky to have had her as a mistress, instead of the master that these unfortunate souls were escaping. After a while, making extremely slow progress getting back to the camp, I insisted on the mother and father taking my horse the rest of the way. With the children on the dead man's horse, the parents on my horse and me holding the reins of both, we finally sighted the cooking fires.

Caleb, ever the kind-spirited friend of slaves, opened his big arms wide to welcome the runaway family, just as he did with the strangers from the Creek nation. It was as if his mission was no longer for himself alone, running from injustice. It was transformed into a march toward something, and it included freedom for us and all whom we encountered. Yet what we had left to cook was not much. Our physical strength was fading by the hour and the cheerful banter that characterized the first few days of our journey was also nearly gone. Generous as he was, Caleb could not make food appear out of thin air, and so our bodies weakened. That night, we shivered in the cold that finally set in for good. Still, our resolve to continue, each day believing we were nearing Mexico, was as strong as ever. I had lost track of the days, but the cold told me it must have been getting late in the month of November. Jumping Ben returned with a few small animals he hunted and the news that he had found the crossing we were hoping for. At daybreak, the whole camp would follow him to the place where a small island in the middle of the river bettered our chances to safely pass to the south bank and on to the next river, the Red River, the border of Texas.

Caleb took me aside and we sat by a small fire that was reduced to mostly glowing embers. It was still giving off warmth, though, which was enjoyed, since I could see my breath in the cold air. "I heard it was pretty rough, finding that family," he said "I'm proud of you, Book."

"I guess I did what I had to do, but... I wish I didn't."

"You mean killing that man?" I looked puzzled because I hadn't told him. "Ben told me."

"Uh huh."

"I have never killed a man, myself," he said. "I guess it's an odd feeling."

"I didn't even hesitate. I didn't even think about it. I knew what I was going to do and I did it."

"Is that wrong?" he asked.

"At first, I was sad over it, thinking I had sinned. I don't think that now, but I'm scared."

"Scared of what?"

"That killing came to me so easily, so naturally"

He just looked at me, finding no words to comfort me. Then he said, "Protecting that family and all of us is what came naturally. Not the killing."

I wanted to tell Misty what had happened to me that day, but she seemed so distant, quiet and frightened that I couldn't find the words to begin. She had been that way since the storm. Though I never mentioned it, I was disappointed that it was not she who had tended to my injury. I could see that she was shaken by the ferocity of the storm. The fact was, though, I couldn't truly depend on her when I needed her assistance the most. Back on the Vanner plantation, I had a very different impression of her.

THE FREEDOM GAME

The confidence, the sense of humor, were hidden beneath her ever-present fear. Still, I didn't want to hold it against her. We were in the midst of a constant storm of uncertainty and discomfort, not just the unole that came and went. Under these circumstances a great deal could be forgiven. Yet, my disappointment was real, and maybe I didn't have to say it for her to know it. Maybe it showed.

The next day, our trip to the crossing spot was agonizingly slow. We had some fifteen 'guests' on foot, including some children. They all followed the wagon at the end of our column. The wagon was also slow, with no road to where we needed to go. Every bump threatened to break a wheel or an axle. Rose amazed me with her skill and strength, but they couldn't make it any faster. At last, we lined up to cross in the order that we had traveled, knowing that the wagon would present the most difficulty.

"Ben, how about some advice for getting the wagon across?" Caleb asked when we were had reached the right place.

I broke into the conversation without waiting for Ben to respond. "Maybe we should unload the wagon first and carry as much as we can on the horses to the other side. That way, we'll lighten the wagon and, if something should happen to it, we'll have at least saved the goods." They looked at each other, then at me. "What?" I said.

They laughed. Caleb rubbed my head, and Ben slapped me on the back. "You were always smart, but when did you grow up, too?" Caleb said. I shrugged my shoulders and grinned.

Ben said, "You're right, Book. Especially the ammunition. We don't want it to get wet, even if it does make it across."

"Then let's get to work," Caleb ordered.

We unloaded everything we could from the wagon and either packed it onto the animals or prepared it to be carried in our arms. The water wasn't deep, only a few feet, but it was icy cold. There was no other way to cross to the island but to wade into it and keep moving, leading the fully packed horses to the island. It was slippery, and the fast moving water made it more treacherous than it looked. One by one, we stepped onto the island, pulling each other and propping each other up. Those on the island helped those in the river to find their footing on dry land. All that remained on the north side of the river were the wagon and the people who had either ridden in the wagon or followed behind it. From the island, I waved to Misty, who had been traveling with Rose. She had gotten off to wait her turn at crossing along with the runaway family and the strangers. Rose repeatedly yelled "Get on up" to her team of horses until, reluctantly, they obeyed her urging to enter the cold, rushing river. Their hooves slid on the slippery rocks as we watched her snap the reins and command them to push forward. They strained to walk, but something held them back. The wagon stopped its progress and sat, as if frozen, in water nearly to the top of the motionless wheels. Nothing Rose could do could make the wagon move. The horses struggled and shivered, making angry, yet pathetic noises, frightened and bewildered that they could not get themselves out of the cold water. We all watched, helplessly.

Making himself heard over the sounds of the flowing water, Caleb called out to Tall Bone and Cotton Hand, "Bone, Cotton can you pull on the horses to get them to move?" They waded in. They pulled as Rose kept up her urging. Still, there was no visible movement.

"It's not the horses. The wagon must be caught on something, Caleb," Tall Bone shouted.

"We have to get the horses out of the water before their legs freeze," Cotton shouted.

"You're right," Caleb answered. "Loosen the harness and..." A loud cracking noise interrupted him. "What was that? Was that the wagon wheel?"

"I don't think so," Tall Bone said. Then another crack was heard. This time, one of our men fell in the same instant.

"Somebody's shooting at us!" Caleb exclaimed. "Everybody get down. Rose, Bone, Cotton, get out of there! Now!"

Tall Bone yanked Rose from the wagon and carried her in his powerful arms to the shore of the island with Cotton Hand close behind. The pops and cracks of gunfire were now all around us. "Get down, I said," Caleb called, "Get down!" to a man who had stood up to see where the shots were coming from. It was too late, though. The man fell to the ground, shot dead.

The enemy revealed themselves to be a posse of what must have been thirty or forty armed men, some shooting, some re-loading. The posse quickly overwhelmed those of us who had not yet crossed to the island, the family, the strangers and Misty, rounding them up on the river bank. There was much noise and confusion, but all I could hear was Misty's panicked voice, screaming my name as she was taken prisoner along with the rest. "Book! Book! Don't let them take me! Help me, Book!"

"I have to get her," I screamed and stood up. Caleb grabbed my arm.

"Get down! You'll be killed before you even reach the water!"

"But they have Misty." I tried to free myself from his grip. Instead, he pulled me back, next to him, pinning me to the ground with his strength and his weight.

"It's done," he said. "They have her. There's no way to get her back. I'm sorry. The best we can do is keep them from crossing to the island." He called out, "Shooters fire back. Make you shots count. Re-loaders, get busy."

In a matter of minutes, our shooters were firing round after round into the oncoming posse. Most shots missed, but a few of the posse fell and the surprise of such an impressive show of force in such a short time had unnerved the posse. It was as though they were facing the fire power of fifty regular guns, thanks to our five-shot revolvers and re-loading teams. The posse fell back, tripping over one another in their haste to get away. They took their captives and fled the scene and were soon as far out of sight as when we first heard their gunshots. Cheers, prayers of thanks and joyful laughter rose from our people. I was not one of those cheering, though. Misty had been among those taken. In that instant, all of the plans we made for a life together in blissful freedom were shattered, and in the midst of the celebration, I felt suddenly alone, utterly and devastatingly helpless. I would have been willing to do anything that would save Misty from her return to slavery. Anything. I even contemplated turning myself over to the posse and resuming my slave life, in order to offer Misty whatever protection from harm I might be able to give. We had escaped once and if I were with her, we could escape again. I had to try, even if it meant death or a life of slavery. I told this to Caleb. His reaction was almost violent.

"Caleb, I have to go back," I said in my most serious voice. Then I shouted, "I have to go back!"

He shouted back. "Go back? What's the matter with you, Book?

"They took Misty. I have to get her back."

"You can't," he said in an understanding tone. "She's gone, Book."

"Maybe if I turn myself over to them, I can do something to protect her, or free her."

"Are you crazy, boy?" he said, impatiently. "Turn yourself to over to what? The chains? The hanging rope? You think you can protect her? Have you forgotten already exactly how unprotected a slave is? You're not turning yourself over to anyone."

"But I have to. I have to."

He grabbed me by both arms. "I'll tell you what. If I see your back as you go north to turn yourself in, I will not hesitate to shoot you square in the middle of it. A good, clean shot to end your madness and spare you the useless suffering that you would bring down on your empty head. Now, I hope you understand me. There is to be absolutely no more talk about any turning yourself, unless you know how to turn yourself and all of us into birds with big wings, so we can fly to Mexico before we all starve to death. I know you had feelings for Misty, but she's gone, boy." Those words kept repeating inside my head. She's gone. Misty is gone. Why didn't I make her cross the river with me? Why didn't I plan for this? If I'm so smart, why did I let this happen? She was the most vulnerable, the one who needed looking after. It was my job to protect her. Now she was in the hands of the slavers. This burden was almost too much for me to carry. They called me a great man. In that moment, I felt neither great, nor a man. I was a weak boy who had let her down when she needed me.

It was Millie who seemed to know what I was going through. Caleb's toughness was meant to keep me focused, of course, but Millie offered me the tenderness of a caring friend. She sought me out when she was told what had happened. She found me standing by the bodies of the two men who had been killed in the battle. I hardly knew them, but I couldn't stop looking at them, as though Misty and I were also among those who were lost that day. "Bookie, I heard about Misty. I'm so sorry. Here. Take a sip." She put a water bag up to my lips. I hadn't realized how thirsty I was until she gave me the water.

"Millie, I didn't save her. I should have."

She shook her head, stroked my face and said, "We're all doing what we can. None of us is perfect. Not even you my brave Book. Not even you." Her words were so real, they felt almost harsh, but the kindness that brought them to her lips, made them soothing to me. We sat there for a while, just being quiet. I was awakened from my thoughts when I heard Caleb ask Ben who he thought it was who attacked us.

"That couldn't have been the posse I expected," Caleb said. "They left without me. If that had been a posse from Money Joe, I'm the one they would have come for, me and the rest of his slaves. Except for a few who were unlucky enough to have been on the north side of the river, behind the wagon, they mostly took the ones who ran away from Creek masters."

"I think you're right," Ben said. "I'm sure the men who attacked us were Creeks. They wanted the runaway strangers. I'm afraid it will get back to the Cherokee Council where we are. We should get started south as soon as we can."

"How's our ammunition?"

"Almost used up. I still have some of what I brought for my musket, but we used up a lot of the pistol supplies fighting off the posse. I don't think we can do much more fighting if another posse attacks. We're also low on food, so we'll have to use the ammunition that's left to hunt."

It was clear that our situation was worse than desperate. Mr. Money Joe's posse could still be coming and we were nearly defenseless against them if they did. We were already hungry all the time, and soon it would be impossible to hunt for more food. Misty was gone, once again a slave. I had killed a man and the guilt was constantly hanging over me. In just the past few days, our chances of actually making it to Mexico became very small. Crossing the river was a goal. It meant that we were beyond the reach of Webb's Bend, that winning our freedom was truly happening. Our plan was fading. It was likely that we would either die in this wilderness, or be caught and returned to slavery. Somehow, I had to find the strength to keep going in spite of everything that had happened. I sensed a familiar, but very unwelcome feeling overwhelm me, the same feeling I used to get when the prison of slavery seemed to be closing in on me. My heart started beating wildly. I had trouble breathing. The world was spinning around me. I thought I would die. I told myself to play the freedom game. I could go anywhere, inside my head, if I got deeply enough into it. Then I would be alright and it wouldn't matter where I was or what was happening. I closed my eyes, but, just as I was deciding where to go, I felt something pulling on me.

"Bookie. Bookie wake up. We have to go. Caleb says everybody on their horses." It was Millie, shaking me. "Didn't you hear him? Come on. We have to go."

Strangely, hearing her voice instantly calmed me down. My heart returned to normal. My vision was clear. I knew I would find a way out of this. I knew I had killed for a reason. I knew there was nothing I could have done to save Misty. Hearing her voice made me strong again. I looked at her. "Millie."

She giggled. "What? Come on. How can you sleep now, anyway?"

"Nothing. Never mind." I smiled to her and went looking for my horse. Not all of the horses had come back. Some had gone back to the other side of the river and were far away.

Cotton rode up to us and pointed to Millie. "You ride with Book."

We climbed onto the horse, Millie in back of me, holding me around my waist. We joined the slow line of walking horses, most carrying two riders. The day was giving way to a magnificently colored sky of pink and gold. There was nothing to eat, so there was no reason to break for supper. We just kept riding into the night. It felt good to have Millie at my back. Though she was usually talkative, she had been quiet that night. I guess she was involved in her own thoughts, or maybe she was as tired as I.

CHAPTER 10

The battle at the Canadian river had changed us, and not only with physical exhaustion. We had gotten away, most of us, with our lives, but with not much more than that. Every mile traveled was harder than the last one. Ben told us that we were getting closer to the next crossing at the Red River, the Texas border. We would have to make a decision to follow the river and approach Mexico from the west, or take our chances on the Chihuahua Trail, cutting through Texas. The Trail was shorter and faster, but some Texans owned slaves, and while there was a question about whether they would want to return us to the Indian Territory, we all agreed that being taken prisoner to be sold in Texas was a real possibility. Reaching the Red River would have another meaning for us, too. Jumping Ben had promised to lead us only as far as the Red River before turning north and heading back to Webb's Bend. Despite the fact that Ben was a wanted man, an outlaw for helping us and killing a slave catcher, he intended to get word to Miss Annie to meet him in order to escape together. The territories of the western United States were big and there would places for them to go to start their lives over. Annie meant everything to Ben and I was sure that nothing could keep him from trying to be with her again. It was pretty certain that he would be leaving, and we would be on our own soon.

As we rode further south, the ground became harder, more rocky. The land was cold and dry. One after another, our horses started coming up lame. Doubling up didn't work anymore, and some of us were now on foot. Our progress was slower than ever. Ben spotted a clearing where huge boulders stood before a low, ridge with some trees. At least this natural wall would provide some protection from the elements. Ben said, "Caleb, I think we should make camp for the night in that clearing." A look of shame and embarrassment came over Ben's face. He spoke haltingly as if the words did not want to leave his mouth. "You're just a few miles from the Red River now and..."

Caleb interrupted him. He could tell, as I could what was coming next. Caleb wanted to make it easier for Ben. "My friend. My dear, dear friend. Your bravery, your..."

It was Ben's turn to interrupt. Ben did not want to be made a fuss over. He held up his hand to stop the speech of gratitude and admiration that Caleb was about to make. "What I have done I wanted to do. I chose this path, freely. Whatever happens now, good or bad, I am glad to have done what was right. For years, Annie and I spoke about slavery, wondering how we could ever help. I looked for such a way. You gave me the way."

Millie asked me, "What are they talking about?"

"Ben promised to lead us as far as the Red River. Since we're almost there, he's going to turn back North."

She got louder. "And leave us here? Are you kidding?"

"He's a free man, Millie."

"But we need him. How will we know where to go?"

"We'll have to manage."

"How can you be so calm?"

"There's nothing we can do about it except thank him for the wonderful things he's done for us."

We reached the clearing. "Caleb," I said, "Millie and I are going to take a look around the trees up there and see if there's any food."

"Good," he replied. "Here," he took the gun from his belt and handed it to me. "That's the last loaded gun. If you see something, don't miss." He chuckled, though it wasn't really very funny.

I gently goaded our tired horse to keep going. We climbed a steep path that lead to the ridge. I guessed that if there was anything worth eating, it would be found in the thick clump of trees that grew along the ridge, overlooking the camp. The horse had found a patch of some vegetation and quietly nibbled. I was about to dismount when we heard a distant rumbling that made Millie and me look at one another, puzzled.

"Is that another storm coming?" she asked.

"The sky is clear," I answered slowly, a feeling of dread building in me, though from what I did not yet know.

"It's getting closer. I think it's coming from over there." She was looking north, the direction our group had just come from. I turned the horse to face it. She found more to nibble on and was content. We were high up enough to see far away and close enough to look down on the camp and hear Ben telling Caleb that he was seeing some movement to the north. The dust was rising in a line, still too far away to see any detail, but enough for Millie and me to know it was headed fast, straight for the camp. Someone was following our trail.

"Can you tell how many there are?" I said. By now we could make out the silhouettes of horses and riders. "We should go warn Caleb."

"He knows." We overheard Caleb telling everyone to keep calm and he would deal with it. Calm wasn't the problem. They were worn out to the bone, with stomachs that had been empty for days. They could hardly move anyway, even if they weren't calm. Besides, I had the only loaded gun. "Here they come," Millie said. "So many."

I later found out that on November 17, 1842, a mere two days after we left Webb's Bend, Mr. Money Joe Vanner had stood before the Cherokee Council in Tahlequah, describing the horrible misfortune that had befallen him. He had come to the Council to make an urgent request for their assistance. He asked that they do whatever may be necessary to apprehend and return his property, to restore order and tranquility for the sake of the whole Cherokee Nation. Word of our escape had spread throughout the Territory, undoubtedly causing Mr. Money Joe great embarrassment, in addition to the economic hardship he was suffering without us. We slaves, of course, were the property in question. But, in making our escape, some were even calling it a revolt. We had completely upended any notion that we were Money Joe's or anyone's property. We had shown the world that we were no one's willing slaves. What we were willing to do was risk our very lives to escape being anyone's slaves. We were also willing to kill to do it. This threatened the fortunes of the wealthiest slaveholders who had the law on their side. However they may have felt about one another in the past, whatever blood feuds had festered between them, protecting the institution of slavery was the most important consideration. It didn't take long for the Council to determine that we were guilty of deliberately depriving Mr. Money Joe of his property, damaging not only him, but stabbing at the very heart of the plantation system and the fortunes that were acquired from its success. They knew full well that we, the slaves, were the primary reason for their financial success. Those of the Council who had so generously benefited from enslaving us had every reason to give Mr. Money Joe all he asked for to get us back, and more. We were to be tracked, caught and forced once again to work for our lawful master. At Fort Gibson, Captain John Drew was given the commission to form and provision an army of 87 Cherokee soldiers to pursue us. More than a local, hired posse, this was a military operation that began the search for us on November 21st. Even with a six day head start, and all the hope in our hearts, there was never really a chance that of any of us would make it to Mexico before being captured by this well-supplied, disciplined force. That knowledge wouldn't have made any difference to us, though. We would have gone anyway.

The riders were Captain Drew's soldiers and they had reached the camp ready for battle, each one brandishing a musket or pistol. They were ordered to spread out and encircle the camp by the Captain, whose drawn sword gleamed in the gold and purple light of the setting sun. Weapon after weapon was aimed with precision at every one in the camp. To resist in any way would mean instant death for all.

Caleb walked, hands raised toward the Captain. "Stop there," the Captain said sharply. "Are you the slave, Caleb?"

"I am Caleb. I was a slave."

"And these are what is left of the slaves who ran away from the Vanner plantation?"

"They were Vanner slaves."

"I am Captain John Drew, commissioned by the Cherokee Council to return you to the Council for justice under the law. I have special orders regarding six of you. The slaves called Caleb, Rose, Cotton Hand, Book Boy, and Tall Bone are wanted for the hanging offense of inciting their fellow slaves to revolt and run away from their lawful master. The Cherokee man called Jumping Ben is wanted for the hanging offense of inciting slaves to revolt and run away from their lawful master. I will add to these charges the murder of two legal slave catchers known to me, whose bodies we found on your trail. If you five come peaceably, the others will be spared execution. Know for a fact that I will shoot if I must."

My heart sank. I was marked for execution by the Cherokee Council. There would be no return to slavery if I were caught, there would be only death. But, if I didn't turn myself in, all of those people would die because of me. As I opened my mouth to identify myself to the Captain, resigned to my fate, Millie placed her fingertips over my mouth. She looked at me with eyes that pleaded for my silence. I did not speak.

Caleb looked up into the eyes of the mounted Captain. "We will come. You need not shoot." The condemned five stepped forward to save the others who looked on, many with grateful tears.

Captain Drew spoke. "I count only five. Who is missing?" He studied his list. "Is it the boy? Book Boy? Where is Book Boy?"

Rose to a step toward the Captain. "Book Boy is dead. He was killed at the river by the Creek posse."

"Very well," he said. Captain Drew had accepted her explanation and I was now dead to the Cherokee Nation.

The soldiers jabbed at them with the barrels of their muskets, some with bayonets, as the five condemned prisoners slid their shackled feet along the hard ground to the wagon that would carry them to their death. Ben recognized one of the soldiers. It was his friend Yellow Tree from Webb's Bend. "Yellow Tree, is that you?" Ben called out.

"Yes, Jumping Ben, it's me. I'm sorry, my friend. I'm a blacksmith, not a soldier. But I needed the money. I'm sorry."

"I understand, Yellow Tree. Tell Annie that I love her." Yellow Tree nodded.

The prisoners were put in the wagon with difficulty because of the irons on their feet. Tall Tree was almost too big for them to maneuver. Eventually, the five stood on the deck of the open wagon just as the darkness of night began spreading over the world. Already, it was difficult to see clearly, but from the wagon, Rose still seemed able to pierce through the trees and the darkness for Millie and me. Staying out of sight, we would never get to say our last goodbyes to her, but we heard her clear, sweet voice, almost like singing. "Don't you worry about me, children," Rose called out. "I'll be fine. I'll be looking down on you, making sure you're alright. I love you and I know you love me." She kissed us both, in the air.

Then, Caleb spoke to all the runaways who, by now, had gathered around the wagon. They stared up at him, waiting for him, their leader, to tell them what to do. "Up until a short time ago, we lived our lives as slaves. We were property, no different to our masters from a tool, or cattle. And yes, I was a slave in my heart. I believed and accepted that this was the life the good Lord had chosen for me. But I see now how very wrong I was to believe this." His voice grew louder. "I was wrong because the Lord didn't just make me to live as a body to do work. Inside, I was someone else, not a slave, not property. I was much, much more than that. In my thoughts, I found that I could be free; free to go where I wanted, do what I wanted. My young brother," he stopped for a moment and smiled. He knew that I was out of sight, but that I was listening to every word. "He calls this the freedom game. To think free, in your mind. It is no game, though. It's real, alright. Those thoughts of freedom were strong enough to make me break those chains for a while, these past weeks we've traveled together. It's as real as anything in this world is real. My hands and feet may be shackled in iron, with a lash on my back and," he paused, "soon a noose on my neck. I know that I am truly free in my heart. Not one of them can take that freedom from me. Not an overseer, not a slave driver, not a master, not even the Cherokee Council with all its laws against me. My freedom in a place they can't touch." He put his hand over his heart. "I may be dressed in chains now, but I will leave this world a free man."

As he spoke, I drew my pistol. I braced my shooting arm with my other arm carefully aiming my gun at the chest of the Captain who stood near Caleb. I had five shots in the gun. I could take the Captain and four more of them down if I aimed well. Maybe Caleb could run. I felt Millie's breath on my neck. "No," she whispered. She gently placed her hand on the top of the gun. I lowered the weapon, knowing she was right. I looked over my shoulder to see her sad eyes, welling up with tears, her head telling me no, telling me it's too late to save them. I positioned our horse to turn to the open field and tried hard to remember the map that Jumping Ben had drawn on his cabin wall as we quietly left.

EPILOGUE

When the War Between the States came, the Cherokee Nation decided to fight on the side of the slave-owning Confederacy. They raised an army, but their heart wasn't in it. Many of the Cherokee soldiers just went back to their homes after a few battles. When the war was nearly over for good, the slave owners told us we were free. Most of the slaves were surprised and didn't know what to do. Some of the former Confederate soldiers, bitter over the outcome of the war, drifted through the Indian Territory, picking deadly fights with the newly freed slaves and forcing themselves on the slave women. The Cherokees tried to protect us, but many freed slaves left to start their own towns, like Tullahassee, where they could build a new life and take care of each other. Funny, throughout my youth, I dreamed more than anyone of leaving Webb's Bend and it was I who returned. Some other freed slaves had remained, mostly to continue working on the same farms where they were born and had toiled for their whole lives. It was all they knew how to do to survive. Still others went north, hearing about opportunities for work and a new, better life. It wasn't that I didn't think I could be successful somewhere else. Maybe I came back because I wanted to prove that I was always good enough, smart enough to be as free as anyone else in Webb's Bend. A part of me hopes that's not the reason, though. I shouldn't have to prove that I deserve to be free. When I was a slave, I was a slave whether I was right or wrong, good or bad. No matter how smart I was, or how good a job I did, or how tall I was or how light or dark my skin was, I was a slave and nothing was going to change that. The same should be true for my freedom. Whether I'm right or wrong, good or bad, smart, slow, tall, short, light skin, dark skin, I don't have to prove anything to show that I'm worthy of being free. So, I hope I didn't stay here to prove anything like that. Now, of course, with my wife, my son and my daughter to protect and provide for, it's not so easy to just pick up and go as it was in my youthful imagination. Yes, I'm bound to stay here, in Webb's Bend, but I thank God it's not the bondage of the lash, of the gun, of the noose. I'm bound to stay by the love of my family, not by the hateful laws that forced me to be someone's property, like an object.

I'm not Book Boy anymore. I'm Bookman Vanner, now. After the War, when I had returned to Webb's Bend, just before Missus died, she told me that I would be needing a last name, now that I was free. She said I should take the name Vanner, since I really was old Money Joe's son, though he would never own up to being my father. My mother, who she didn't know, died giving birth to me. Missus said that when I was old enough to be without a wet nurse, it was Money Joe's idea to have me live on the plantation and learn to read. If all that is true, and I have no reason to doubt it, I guess everybody was kind of right about me. Money Joe was part Cherokee and part white. Judging from my skin color, my mother must have been a slave of African descent. That makes me African, Cherokee and white. I don't feel any different, though, knowing all that.

I write for newspapers and magazines, now, telling folks about what happens here in the Indian Territory, sometimes real, sometimes fiction, sometimes a little of both. I even send my stories to the papers back east. Who knows, maybe one of those New York publishers will want to print this story. I'm not just writer, though. I have to do other things too, to keep body and soul together. For instance, I was recently hired as the clerk at Grady's general store, part-time since there isn't as much business as before the war. As a boy, I had been there so many times for Missus, I knew where everything was and how much it cost already. Sometimes, if I need extra money, I even work at the Vanner place where I used to be a slave, but now, at the end of the day, instead of sleeping on the floor of a crowded slave house, I go home to my family. We live in Jumping Ben and Miss Annie's old cabin in the woods. It was deserted for years and we needed a place to live. We made it bigger with another room for sleeping, but I think Ben and Annie would be happy that we live there. They had no kids of their own and I think they would like it a lot.

So, here we stand, my young son and I, watching solemnly as the last grave stone is set in its place by the men I hired. I want him to understand so much. I want their story to show him that an act of true bravery doesn't always end in victory, not right away. I want him to see that sometimes even the most desperate struggle is still worth the fight, even when all reason is shouting that the fight can't be won and you give it everything you have, anyway. I understand that now. I wasn't always so certain of this. I truly hope he'll read this when he's older, but not too old not to find it's lessons useful in his life. It's not that I'm blind to my heroes' faults. Heroes have faults. They were flesh and blood people and real people are never perfect. Still, all these years later, as I picture them in my mind's eye, they may as well be giants, standing taller in spirit than anyone I have known since. They deserve to be honored and what they did deserves to be remembered.

"You know, before there was a Confederate Army, before there was a Union Army, before there was a War Between the States, before the was a President Lincoln, before there was an Emancipation Proclamation, these people were reaching out for their freedom."

"Look, Pa, It says C-A-L-E-B! Caleb! That's my name!"

"Yes! You're right, Caleb. Good reading, boy. The man who is buried here was called Caleb and that's where I got the name for you. I wanted you to have the name of the finest person I ever knew."

"Tell me about him, Pa. What was he like?"

I looked up and saw my lovely wife, Millie and my tall, beautiful daughter, Rose, standing next to us. "It's kind of a long story, Caleb, but a good one." I hugged and kissed Millie and Rose.

Rose studied the freshly set gravestones. "Look Pa, one of them is named Rose. I want to hear the story, too, Pa." Millie just smiled.

ABOUT THE AUTHOR

R. A. Blumenthal was born in Brooklyn, NY and raised mainly in Amityville, NY. He holds a Bachelor of Arts degree from SUNY College at Old Westbury and a Master of Science degree from Long Island University, where he studied Counseling. Licensed as both a mental health counselor and a school counselor, Mr. Blumenthal is the originator of a cognitive behavioral treatment called Rational Suggestion Therapy, about which he has written for professional journals. In 2003, he was awarded a United States patent for his invention of a computer hypnosis method. A lifelong lover of history, Mr. Blumenthal endeavors to find the more human aspects of historic events. He currently resides on Long Island, NY with his wife Linda Blumenthal and their children, Sarah and Emily.

CPSIA information can be obtained
at www.ICGtesting.com
Printed in the USA
LVHW031133271019
635473LV00002B/374/P

Ancient Algorithms
by Katrine Øgaard Jensen, with Sawako Nakayasu, Aditi Machado,
CAConrad, Baba Badji, Paul Cunningham, and Ursula Andkjær Olsen

An utterly singular project from National Translation Award winner, Katrine Øgaard Jensen.

Equal parts exercise and exorcism, *Ancient Algorithms* recasts translation as an endlessly generative art form unto itself. Poet-translator Katrine Øgaard Jensen mistranslates, rewrites, and remixes her award-winning translations of Ursula Andkjær Olsen's poetry based on a series of self-imposed rules and rituals in collaboration with poets Sawako Nakayasu, Aditi Machado, CAConrad, Baba Badji, Paul Cunningham, and Ursula Andkjær Olsen herself.

A project that engages head-on with traditional classifications of "original," "translation," and even "poem," *Ancient Algorithms* is destined to be a cult favorite of experimental poets and a foundational text for poetry and translation workshops alike.

Katrine Øgaard Jensen is the incoming Executive Director of the American Literary Translators Association. An award-winning Danish poet and translator based in New York, she is a recipient of the National Translation Award in Poetry, Kenyon Review's Peter Taylor Fellowship, and the Danish Arts Foundation's Young Artistic Elite Fellowship among many honors and distinctions. Previously, Katrine taught Creative Writing and Literary Translation at Columbia University, where she also served as Acting Director of Literary Translation. She has also worked as the Executive Administrator and Project Manager at the Author's Guild and Programs Manager at the Council for European Studies.

Sarabande Books
978-1-956046-43-4 / Trade paperback / 120 pgs.
On sale 9/30/2025
$17.95

For marketing and publicity, please contact:
michelle@sarabandebooks.org

ANCIENT ALGORITHMS

KATRINE ØGAARD JENSEN

ANCIENT
ALGORITHMS

with

URSULA ANDKJÆR OLSEN
SAWAKO NAKAYASU
ADITI MACHADO
PAUL CUNNINGHAM
BABA BADJI
CACONRAD

SARABANDE BOOKS

Publisher's Cataloging-In-Publication Data
(Provided by Cassidy Cataloguing Services, Inc.).

[PCIP TK]

Cover by Sarah Flood-Baumann.
Interior design by Kit Schluter.

Printed in USA.
This book is printed on acid-free paper.
Sarabande Books is a nonprofit literary organization.

This project is supported in part by an award from the National Endowment for the Arts.
The Kentucky Arts Council, the state arts agency, supports Sarabande Books with state tax
dollars and federal funding from the National Endowment for the Arts.

Fellow Poets, translation weaves, it weaves solidarity.

DON MEE CHOI,
"Darkness—Translation—Migration"

TABLE OF CONTENTS

KATRINE ØGAARD JENSEN

A NOTE TO THE READER

> like a suction in there
> of who owes what
>
> and who owes what to whom
>
>
> (nature as something you don't owe anything
> anything as something you don't owe anything)
>
> URSULA ANDKJÆR OLSEN, *My Jewel Box*
> translated by Katrine Øgaard Jensen

To whom do the poems in this book belong? They are ours and not-ours, evolving via the various vessels (poet-translators) through which they transition.

The starting point for these collaborations were my English translations

of the Danish poet Ursula Andkjær Olsen's works *Det 3. årtusindes hjerte* (*Third-Millennium Heart*), *Udgående fartøj* (*Outgoing Vessel*), and *Mit smykkeskrin* (*My Jewel Box*), all published by Action Books. Together, the works form a trilogy—a "fairy tale of the universe" investigating grief, bodies, motherhood, and the physical and economic inequities of modern planetary life.

In order to capture the spirit of these works—which begin with small motifs and expand over time into a text that continues to grow—I chose to let the English versions evolve in translation as well. This meant purposefully creating new possibilities for language and imagery rather than confining the text to something that could only lose in translation. Olsen not only supported this approach, but enthusiastically participated in rewriting her own texts in English, imagining how I might translate her work. The resulting translations became hybrids: my English voice imitating Olsen's Danish voice, and Olsen, in turn, imitating my English voice imitating her Danish voice.

Somewhere in this process, I suggested escalating the translations further by deliberately "mistranslating" certain poems together and allowing them to evolve beyond the books themselves. The *Berkeley Poetry Review*, *Ordkonst*, the *Kenyon Review*, and *BOMB* generously hosted these experiments in translation, and I invited more collaborators to join the evolution.

In some cases, I would invite a collaborator—a fellow poet-translator—to pick a poem from Olsen's trilogy to transwrite (or mistranslate) based on a set of self-imposed rules. The collaborator would then send me their mistranslation along with the rules they created to write their poem. Next, I would mistranslate their poem based on my own set of rules. Once finished, I would send my mistranslation and rules back to the collaborator, and we would continue the process of sending poems back and forth between us, creating new rules with each mistranslation.

In other instances, especially when collaborating with Olsen on corrupting her poems, I would open the collaboration with a mistranslated text myself, sometimes with a poem-to-poem approach and other times with a book-to-poem transritual or trilogy-to-poem transwriting game.

The poems are credited to the individuals who composed them, with each section credited to the collective they arose from. Each poem is, to borrow an expression from Alejandra Pizarnik in Cole Heinowitz's translation, not necessarily an expression of being but rather a memorial for a moment of fusion.

FOR YOUR CONSIDERATION

> Consider this an egoism-exorcism, always fascinated by selfishness itself,
> hence the necessity for a ceremony with selfishness and my me-wagon, in
> shiny velvet leading the holy procession.

URSULA ANDKJÆR OLSEN, *Third-Millennium Heart*
translated by Katrine Øgaard Jensen

Consider this: Ursula Andkjær Olsen doesn't view her poetry as original work, but rather a translation of an idea—an idea of which she is simply the first translator.

Consider this: All writing is translation.

Consider this: All literary translators are writers.

Consider this: Translation = collaboration = a loss of control = a trust exercise.

Consider this a celebration of the undead authors who encourage their own dismemberment, who happily break off a limb and hand it to the writers transcreating their work.

Consider this the Uncanny Silicon Valley of uneconomical writing, of unproductive translations that increase the distance between reader and "original."

Consider this: All writing is collaboration—between the author and their influences, the specter of other authors and translators haunting each text.

Consider: alle og ingen kar er forbundne—all and no vessels are connected.

I PLACE THE WORLD

SAWAKO NAKAYASU & KATRINE OGAARD JENSEN

rummet
med fire vægge
en terning af let støvet luft inde i kroppen
hele jorden
med øst, vest, syd, nord
som en gyrokugle indeni
i sin egen ligevægt

cellerne der samler sig i deres
kæder, kranse, bånd

***

holde ånden inde
tvinge den til at blive inde i kroppen
trods det kropslige ubehag
trods det nærmest uendelige kropslige ubehag

jeg stiller kroppen ind i verden
og trækker vejret ind
jeg stiller verden ind i kroppen
og puster vejret ud
det er det, jeg gør
jeg er

sørgekrop
vredeskrop
glædeskrop
kærlighedskrop

jeg identificerer mig med alt, med

(ild, vand, jord, luft)

URSULA ANDKJÆR OLSEN

translated by Katrine Øgaard Jensen

two poems from *My Jewel Box*

the room
with its four walls
a cube of light dust and air inside the body
all of earth
with east, west, south, north
like a gyrosphere inside
in its own equilibrium

cells assembling in their
chains, wreaths, bonds

* * *

to keep the spirit inside
force it to stay inside the body
despite physical discomfort
despite almost endless physical discomfort

i place the body inside the world
and breathe in
i place the world inside the body
and breathe out
that is what i do
i am

griefbody
ragebody
joybody
lovebody

i identify with everything, with

(fire, water, earth, air)

SAWAKO NAKAYASU

RULE: ONE POEM INFECTS ANOTHER.

the body is a room
with its fourbody wallbodies
this   is what i do
breathe out

a cube of lightgrief   bodydust   and rage
air   inside the spiritbody
all of earth
breathe out

eastbody westbody southbody nobody
like a gyrosphere joybody lovebody inside
its own body equilibrium

cells assembling world inside the body
bodychains bodywreaths bodybonds
i place the world
i place the body inside the breathing world out

5

KATRINE ØGAARD JENSEN

RULE: NOW REWRITE FROM THE PERSPECTIVE OF
THE WOMAN IN THE CHAIR OF PETER BLUME'S 1932
PAINTING *LIGHT OF THE WORLD.*

i worship in technicolor
with my despairbody chairbuddy
this   is what i do
look up

a sphere of lightgrief   bodydust   and a wish:
my hand   inside the ventriloquist
release the dummy
look up

opalbody celestitebody tourmalinebody topaz
like a crystalline joyosphere shimmering inside
its own electric equilibrium

particles moving world inside the light
windchains sunwreaths coalbonds
i place the light
i place the world inside the light and look

RULE: NOW COPY THE WORDS IN REVERSE ORDER.
ADJUST.

look—
and light—
the inside
world

the place   i light
the place   i coal

bonds sunwreaths
wind chains light
the inside world—
moving—
particles

equilibrium electric
own its inside shimmering

joyosphere
crystalline
alike:

topaz
tourmalinebody
celestitebody
opalbody
uplookdummy

the release
ventriloquist—

the inside hand my wish: a—
and bodydust

lightgrief
of sphere a—

uplook
do i—
what is this—
chairbuddy despairbody my—
with technicolor in—
worship i—

RULE: NOW FEED THE LINES TO AN AI IMAGE GENER-
ATOR AND DESCRIBE THE IMAGES IT PRODUCES.

/imagine the inside world:

A slender, black castle in a gray sky. Spires like dull medieval daggers.
Behind it: an infrastructure of stairs obscured by clouds. In front: a white-
cloaked person under an archway. There is another person closer to the
viewer in a black suit, their back turned. Both faces are hidden, both
bodies turned not toward each other but toward a large sunset-orange
sphere. In the background, barely noticeable, there is a smaller orange
sphere in the open doorway of the castle. As if to say: Whatever it is
you're looking for, it already exists in this world.

/imagine bonds sunwreaths wind chains light:

A golden horizon above sapphire waters. On the shore, distorted wind
turbines dance like nightmare sylphs, a volcanic complex erupts behind
them. Above it all, a symbol in the dark-turquoise sky: a glowing Celtic
circle framing an enormous volcano at its blazing mouth, revealing that
the sky is not the sky at all. I ask the AI to upscale the image, and now
everything is an abstract painting. Now the wind turbines are Blair
Witch sticks, or twisted chromosomes, propelling upward to merge with
whatever world the glowing circle offers.

/imagine joyosphere crystalline:

Four images of shapes, their colors somewhere between harlequin and
crystal opal. 1. Beams, almost like refraction of light through a prism,
but messy, not a rainbow. 2. A chevron with an octahedron at its center
and a beam blazing upward to something glowing out of frame. 3. A
bubble containing sideways pyramids inside another bubble. 4. A crystal
in the shape of a hot-air balloon: a hopeful escape à la early Midlake.

WHEN THE BEGINNING FEELS LIKE AN ENDING, THERE ARE SIGNS

PAUL CUNNINGHAM & KATRINE OGAARD JENSEN

URSULA ANDKJÆR OLSEN

from *Mit smykkeskrin*

alderen, det kick indeni den giver

hvad kan jeg sætte ind
imod det

jeg bliver rig og hul som
rum der opstår af ikke-rum
til sidst bliver jeg så stor at jeg dør
til sidst bliver jeg så uendelig at

hjertet der imploderer

.

så stor
enorm
der er en scene derinde
der står disse figurer på den
dukker, brikker
en relation
en række relationer
de samme relationer som finder sted udenfor
dvs. man tager alle relationerne
og de situationer de befinder sig i
og sætter dem ind i den pågældende person
gentager hele scenen/
livet indeni

det kræver et stort indre
det kræver et indre der udvider sig konstant

13

URSULA ANDKJÆR OLSEN
translated by Katrine Øgaard Jensen
from *My Jewel Box*

my age, the kick inside that it brings

what can i deploy
against it

i'm becoming rich and hollow like
spaces originated in non-spaces
finally becoming so big that i die
finally becoming so infinite that

the heart that implodes
.

so big
enormous
there is a stage in there
with figurines on it
dolls, game pieces
a relation
a row of relations
the same relations that take place outside
i.e. you take all the relations
and the situations they're in
place them in the person concerned
and repeat the entire scene/
life inside

it takes a large interior
it takes an interior that constantly expands

14

RULE: PLACE THE POEM IN THE PERSON CONCERNED AND REPEAT THE SITUATION.

my number comes, like a megakick

how can I
position myself

as if I am nutrientempty
my interior originated from nothing
this is my grandiose ending
this is my grandiose infinity

my pulmonary attack

now we enter
my new growth stage
the stage is a stage
[*I join the cast as Katrine*]
I am no Katrine-doll
I am no doll, I am Katrine
a row of relations
familiar exterior relations
i.e. Paul has taken all the relations
and the situations of place
and entered the person concerned
only to repeat the entire scene
new interiority

new interiority requires grandiose infinity
I have become what takes an interior

KATRINE ØGAARD JENSEN

RULE: NOW TAKE THE POEM ON A VIRTUAL TOUR
OF ROSENBORG CASTLE, HOME TO DENMARK'S CROWN
JEWELS.

this is my grandiose beginning

my interior institution
of absolute monarchy

originated from nothing
now I have a little bit

of everything, such as

700 objects in ivory and amber*
ceilings with paintings of chubby angelic children**

the umbilical cords of my heirs in 8 silver boxes***

1 planetarium 1 eclipsarium
scepter / orb / anointment jar****

now we enter
the winter room garden room
marble room dark room
the latter in which the poem finds
display cabinets with wax busts
each a direct cast of the person portrayed

it is a portrait tradition no longer in use

---

*   gifts from foreign princes in return for white hunting falcons
**   and Bacchus in the ceiling of my glass cabinet
***   plus my own fetal membranes in 1 silver box
**** not to be used until my castrum doloris; the coffin will wear my crown

they are made from life and death masks:
the queen and prince were both alive
while the bust of the king wasn't made
until he was a corpse

RULE: NOW TAKE A POEM TO SAINT MARY'S GATE AND LEAVE A POEM BEHIND.

D

R

A

W

I

N

G

T

K

when the beginning feels like an ending, there are signs

and red mothers who move
beyond sign activity

originator
she is cloaked in such

such everything

all that swims Saint Joseph's Lake
orbs and branches, ideas of children

snaking 8s, side to side purgatorio
two orbs, two eyes purgatorio
round, round, round

entrance denied
at Saint Mary's Gate
forbidden water forbidden bodies
she is pushing through anyway
busting through, waving bloodstained arms
yet another red mother emerges

like an illegal procedure
she's wearing her death mask for life
only queen standing motherfuckers
no bust, but she is busting
she is bursting from his remains

she is the poem she leaves behind

RULE: NOW USE THE POEM AS A PUPPET AND
REWRITE FROM THE PERSPECTIVE OF RAINER MARIA
RILKE'S PUPPETEER ANGEL IN THE FOURTH DUINO
ELEGY.

I angel at the beginning and ending
of the premeditated activities you call life
and yes, there are signs

that I angel above you
beyond language
in the interval between world and game

I jolt life into your hard husk
like an illegal procedure
that lasts your lifetime
except the law is on my side

this celestial body of content
is denying you entrance
to anything real

nothing is what it really is
everything is what I say it is

I am the original hyperstition
the cosmic apparatus
everything that remains
in the world you leave behind

WE MUST BANISH THE INSTRUCTIONS OR BECOME THEM

THREE RITUALS

CAConrad & Katrine Ogaard Jensen

KATRINE ØGAARD JENSEN

RETRANSLATING POETRY WITH RUNES
A RITUAL FOR POET-TRANSLATORS

after CAConrad

1. Take a pair of scissors and a piece of paper, and cut out twenty-four equal-sized squares. On each square, draw one of the twenty-four letters of the runic alphabet called Elder Futhark. Or obtain a set of runes.

2. If the runes are flat, such as paper, ceramic, or wood runes, lay them all facedown on a table. If they are round stone runes, keep them in a bag.

3. Clear a space on the table in front of you and lay a piece of white paper or a white cloth on it. Choose a book or a poem that you've translated and place it next to the white surface. I chose my English translation of Ursula Andkjær Olsen's *Outgoing Vessel.* Ask the runes: "How can I translate this work again?" and draw three runes onto the white surface. I drew ᛉ, Algiz, first; ᛚ, Laguz, second; and finally ᛈ, Perthro—all upright.

4. Interpret the runes. For this retranslation ritual, how you choose to interpret the runes is personal and entirely up to you. You can research the traditional names and/or meanings of each runic character, or you can intuit an interpretation based on the visual appearance and energy of each rune.

5. Give the runes your undivided attention. In Norse mythology, in order to receive the secrets of the runes, the god Odin pierced himself with a sword and hung from the tree of life, Yggdrasil, for nine days and nights. You don't have to hang upside down—you can go for a walk with a rune in your pocket or sit somewhere quiet and observe each rune. Let the runes serve as your medium for poetry by listening as they speak to you, one by one, in the language of inspiration.

Y, Algiz, the rune of defense and protection, guided me toward *Outgoing Vessel*'s reoccurring image of the orb. I found every instance of an orb—literal as well as metaphorical—in the book and wove these together, creating one long text. Then I highlighted my favorite parts of the text, cut them out, and rearranged them into a poem. When invoking the water rune ᚱ, Laguz, I repeated the same procedure with images of water/rivers/lakes/streaming. I let some of the orb images spill into the second poem by transforming them into water, and I let the flow of the second text dictate its own course. The final character, ᚲ, Perthro, the rune of mystery and chance, guided me to merge the two previous poems and run them through several online poetry generators. I wrote the third poem with lines that emerged from the generators.

Y
to send off the hating i:

board the orb in a closed circuit /orb *so that when evening slaughters*
me and eats me and   finds the orb, it will never find it   so that when
i slaughter myself every evening and eat   the meat and find the orb, I
will never find it   evening slaughters me and eats me   and leaves the
orb in the dark   on a big, smooth floor, covered in sleek   orbs   there
stands the human /the orb   devour all meat and expose the bones /the
orb   roll a burning wheel down a hill like a solar symbol   /orb   board
the orb   buckle in   and whatever you want   a desert   sarcophagus   the
orb   the dead   *you can buy and suck on*

↾
in the sarcophagus lies

the foundation of all future life   in still water   i wish i were born still
swaddled in delicate   silk crepe woven souls   i am a stonehard water-
bearer   i am a stonehard water-bearer   i am a stonehard water-bearer
in one motion the desert can be covered in water   just letting you know
water ALL THE WAY   washing   massaging   touching   cradling   strong
BUT smooth   light BUT cold   *a lake-thing inside me, a blue/clear rise*
look into your eyes and see the streaming   talk yourself into seeing the
streaming   suffering is the source   alienation is the mouth   suffering is
the source   alienation is the mouth   i mix the desert with crystal-clear
water   and mold a new human out of the clay

⤙
i water myself into you

wish i were strong BUT smooth like a hill   i'll never find the sarcophagus
and you want the sarcophagus   /orb in the dark   eat me and see the clay
the orb in the orb   a solar symbol massaging your future life   alienation
is the hating you want: devour my eyes and eat me and suck on the orb
in the water   suck on the motion of life   light   i wish i wish i   wish
i wish   to board the dark   on a blueclear day

25

DAGAZ DAYS
A (SOMA)TIC POETRY RITUAL

Please do this ritual for 9 days.

Before going to sleep, wet your finger with your tongue and draw the Dagaz rune on all your doors, on your notebooks where you write your poems, on your forehead, and over and over again over your heart for protection, yes, but also for a portal we will open to the Sun when we wake.

In the morning, draw Dagaz on your forehead and rise to watch the sunrise. Consider the light taking 9 minutes to travel through outer space from the Sun to our planet, where our bodies are waiting to absorb and activate! Write notes in your notebook as fast as you can that will be shaped into a poem at the end of the ritual.

Later in the day, estimate sunrise somewhere else on the planet, then locate an outdoor public webcam to watch the sunrise. Tokyo, Berlin, Istanbul, Los Angeles, or other locations, but choose a different location for 9 days to watch the sunrise. Draw Dagaz on your forehead while watching, then write in your notebook as fast as possible for the poems. Here is a webcam sample from Melbourne, Australia: https://www.youtube.com/watch?v=l_8DrACHpwY. You can easily find outdoor and public webcams on every continent and nearly every country.

After watching online, go out for a walk. Find one small object on your walk that can easily fit in your hand, but collect these objects each day.

At the end of your 9 days, take your 9 objects from your walks and put them in a hat, then walk forward in a straight line while throwing them over your shoulders behind you onto the floor. Only look where they land once you are finished. Consider how the objects fell on the floor to be a map for you to follow.

Now, walk alongside the 9 strewn objects, narrating your interpretation of this map aloud. Take notes for a poem.

Walk alongside the map again, singing its story as loud as possible, then sit and write.

The 3rd walk is silent, caressing places on your body corresponding to each of the 9 objects. Take more notes for a poem.

Draw Dagaz on your forehead before going to sleep. Wake, draw Dagaz on your forehead, then watch the sunrise and write one more time for your poem. Then, read your notes to find the words to shape your poem.

go ahead
call me a
child for
asking
is there
no war
somewhere
instead of this
daily butterfly
fighting
suck of
fan blade
you should
break up is my only
relationship advice
on the
way to
slaughter
pigs on
truck pass
deer with
broken neck
where love
is merely an
afterthought
we must banish
the intrusions or
become them

KATRINE ØGAARD JENSEN

TRANSLATING GRIEF
WITH RELIC TECHNOLOGIES

til min far

1. Find a place to sit in nature. Take this time to think of a loved one whose death you are grieving: This ritual is devoted to them.

2. For inspiration and communication, trace the rune Ansuz ᚨ over your mouth. Take deep breaths. Now search your mind for a technological relic that evokes nostalgia and reminds you of your loved one. What constitutes a relic is up to you; it will depend on your age and your interpretation of the word. Make arrangements to borrow or obtain the relic if it is not already in your possession.

3. Engage with your relic for as long as it takes to establish a connection to the memory of your loved one. Sing along to it, speak to it, move around with it, press all the buttons, sit with it and remember. Translate your experience into notes for a poem. Return to the relic four times over a period of at least four days, take notes for your poem each time. If your loved one comes to you in a dream or otherwise feels present during this period, take notes. Beware of false communications or misinterpretations that may occur during the period; take your time to translate with honesty and thought.

4. After your fourth session with the relic, go back outside and think of your loved one once again. Breathe. Observe nature's ancient technologies. Write down what you see.

5. Create a poem from your notes and read it aloud: a voicemail from your mouth to the Otherworld.

PLAYING MYST WITH A GHOST ONE WEEK IN SPRING

Seagulls swirl in pixels | above giant metal gears | on this speculative

future island | of 1993 | i used to do the pointing | while you did all the
clicking | in sylvan steampunk surroundings | of cozy disquiet | mirrored
by the way you roll | your ghost eyes at me | as i click closed doors that
refuse to open | on a rocket ship | a colossal tree | a clock tower in the
water | Time stands still here | the daylight never changes | you used to
keep notes for us | and now i see why | It is windy on Myst island | and i
don't know where to turn | i click to press a button | by an underground
pool | it could reveal something | but really does nothing | i press other
buttons | turn multiple wheels | take elevators and stairs | to more deserted
spaces | i do meet a man | trapped inside a book | and another | more
hysterical man | trapped inside a second book | Meanwhile | in the real
world | bright grass pierces | a fallen chicken-wire snowman | In the real
world | forsythias lose their gold | The pollinators are here | the scythe-
headed wisteria buds dying | to bloom

WIT IS YOU WHO CORRUPT
MY RAYLESS CORPUS

ADITI MACHADO & KATRINE OGAARD JENSEN

URSULA ANDKJÆR OLSEN

from *Mit smykkeskrin*

så står jeg klar iført

kæde
ring
krone

det landskab
et menneskeligt sted
et umenneskeligt sted mellem bakkerne
strækkende slimhinder og muskler til det yderste
trækkende slimhinder og muskler
bindevæv sammen
om det indeni

(imødegå atrofi)
(omgå) (omstyrte)
(pumpe friskt blod ud i kæder, kranse, bånd)
.

en muslingeskal beklædt med
ingenmor
en muslingeskal beklædt med
allemor

URSULA ANDKJÆR OLSEN

translated by Katrine Øgaard Jensen
two poems from *My Jewel Box*

i stand ready donning a

chain
ring
crown

that landscape
a human place
an inhuman place between the hills
stretching mucous membranes and muscles to the limit
pulling mucous membranes and muscles
connective tissue together
around what's inside

(counter atrophy)
(circumvent) (overthrow)
(pump fresh blood out into chains, wreaths, bonds)
.

a sea shell lined with
mother of nothing
a sea shell lined with
mother of everything

PROCESS:

1. I make my computer count the number of words in the poem on page 187: it is 66.

2. I decide I will translate this poem with the help of a book I keep meaning to read but never manage to finish. It will be like a dictionary. I try a few books of this sort on my shelves and settle on Michel Serres's *The Five Senses*, translated from French into English by Margaret Sankey and Peter Cowley. It has a chapter (unread by me) called "Boxes" which seems apt to translate a poem from a book called *My Jewel Box*.

3. I count the number of pages in this chapter: it is 67. If I cheat and count the seven lines of text on the sixty-seventh page as part of the sixty-sixth, I can translate each word of Olsen-Jensen's poem using one page of Serres-Sankey-Cowley's prose.

4. I decide I will cheat.

5. I write each successive word of the poem on the top righthand corner of the chapter, with the last word ("everything") straddling the gutter across the last two pages.

6. A page at a time, I drift toward a phrase (sometimes just a word)—never reading the entire text—by seduction or by chance. I am not permitted to drift ahead until I have chosen a definition for the word inscribed in the righthand corner. In this way, I translate "i" as "I have been tasting the sun," "stand" as "the location's exact acoustic properties," and so on. This takes quite a long time, several morning hours on October 10, another hour on a flight from Minneapolis to Boise on October 14.

7. I end up with 262 words of plausible prose. I had hoped for a multiple of 6, if not precisely 666.

8. $262 + 66 = 328$. Also, not a multiple of 6. But this is the constraint. I rewrite the bibliomantically arrived-at prose into poetry that sounds, I think, somewhat like Olsen-Jensen but also a lot like me; and also, I suppose, Serres-Sankey-Cowley. This poem is composed of 328 words.

i am tasting the sun
i am tasting location's exact
acoustic properties

my speech, anesthetized by   *debt*
my speech, anesthetized by   *anchorites*
my speech, anesthetized by   *reclusive scholars*
and the dead who gaze at the theater
that is my mother's womb

thus do i exist

thus do i enter the interstice and translation
of this word: economics

it is my strategy
my politics
my illusory science

it is my corpse consulting an ancient algorithm
it is my corpse consulting articles and theses and academic journals

now i am doped on knowledge i would like to pass on

i would like to pass on my tastes and perfumes like a network of tombs

i would like to pass on a single sentence

i would like to pass on the drone of poetic stanzas
of houses and prisons and infernos and ships
on the fringes of distant galaxies and their cities and posters
and medicines

but this flow encounters obstacles

i do not know if

language must be paid for
it is barely audible

the wind's currents stir my body's tissues
which the generalized eardrum
located in the vase of my swollen belly
channels into the uterus and   the world
its box, its ear, its mouth
resounds

and the monads conjure wings
on the verge of being torn apart

and sensation, a black box
hard and soft
soft and hard
descends to the underworld

this is how death composes
the insufferable law
of maximum output

the ordeal of being born
it is the same thing

it is music's unstable and rare equilibrium and my body proliferating
leftwards
through touch

now i am empty space and note combined
skin to the outside world, mucus to the inside

i am twittering and birdsong
under surveillance

i open my dwelling so brutally
i open the vineyards and the tufts of thyme
i overcome the roaring of lions
the furor of the bacchantes

so the long parasitic chains demolish
one dark threshold after another

PROCESS:

1. I spend a lot of time listening to various metal bands and thinking about (despairing over) how to mistranslate Machado's poem.

2. I decide to cut away everything in Machado's process description and poem that doesn't sound metal.

3. I make a list of metal and metal-adjacent song titles that feature (to stay within the jewel box theme) precious stones, metals, or minerals.

4. I create a cut-up poem mashing up Machado's lines with some of the song titles and rewrite/mutate the lines as I see fit. Song titles quoted: Ennio Morricone and Metallica, "The Ecstasy of Gold"; Thin Lizzy, "Emerald"; Judas Priest, "Diamonds and Rust"; DragonForce, "City of Gold"; Quiet Riot, "Metal Health (Bang Your Head)"; Iron Maiden, "The Alchemist"; Slayer, "Metal Storm/Face the Slayer"; Death, "Crystal Mountain"; Iron Maiden, "Rainbow's Gold"; Blue Öyster Cult, "Heavy Metal: The Black and Silver"; Disturbed, "Serpentine"; Judas Priest, "Metal Gods."

5. I edit the poem until the character count equals exactly 666.

i had hoped for a network of tombs   a multiple of 6   if not precisely

666   i am tasting the ecstasy of gold silver platinum palladium   *my speech, anesthetized by emerald   my speech, anesthetized by diamonds and rust   and the dead who gaze at the rhodium   that is my mother's womb*   thus do i exist: thus do i enter the city of gold   conjure wings on the verge of being torn apart   and pray for my metal health   now i am music's unstable and rare equilibrium   now i am empty space and note combined   watch me as i descend to the underworld   one rayless level after another   as i find the alchemist / face the slayer   & bind him with chains to the crystal mountain: it is my strategy   my currency   my rainbow's gold   it is my corpse corrupting an ancient algorithm   it is my corpse corrupting the black & silver   serpentine science of metal gods

PROCESS:

1. I attend the persistent *em*s and *um*s of Jensen's poem. This poem's mettle is unstable music. Unstable mu-sic = sic um = a sick hum.

2. I go backward through the text in 6-syllable lines arranged in tercets. 6 + 6 + 6 = 18.

o silver serpent of
signs, it is you who cor-
rupt my rayless corpus

you who chain me to this
gilded algorithm
i ascend the crystal

mountain, you bind me to
its alchemical will
i ascend the under

world, you conjure a ripped
equilibrium, i
enter your lucent crypt

on the verge of being,
now i am and i am
the unstable and the

rare and thus do i rust
in your recombinant
gaze, thus do i multi-

ply six and speech, i ir-
radiate your network,
i aestheticize your

metal womb, o sick hum
i sought you out and you
went platinum on me

PROCESS:

1. Machado's poem reads like a song, so I decide to write a misread lyrics version (in which, for instance, "the underworld" = "the underworm" / "metal womb" = "metal wombat" / "sick hum = sick humanoid").

2. I listen to the song "11 Dreams" by the Danish metal band Mercenary and decide to write down any details I remember from eleven dreams I've recently had, after which I infuse my dreams with the misread version of Machado's poem.

the more i try to move
my corpse across the earth
the closer i am to an end

we speak the vernacular of believer
as we mount the underworm
its infinite body reaching far-out conclusions

i am a metal wombat managed by Justin Trudeau
i am a sick humanoid late for my math test

enter my lucent cubicle & watch me irradiate your neurons
laud me as i conjure a ripped equinox
a meteor wonderland of sabotage and aesthetics

everyone i love is counting on me
everyone i love is covered in blood
everyone is waiting at the end of a flight

o sandperson simulator of realities
i possess a metamorphic eyeball
i can explode things with my hands
but when will you ever reveal in a dream
the alchemy of finding my airport gate

o singer of silver truths
i am on the verge of seeing
the unstable and the rare
your crimson genealogy

COMPROMISED INFRASTRUCTURE

URSULA ANDKJÆR OLSEN & KATRINE OGAARD JENSEN

Det 3. årtusindes hjerte er et
sted med mange kamre,

kompliceret væsen med broer og passager til at
transportere legemer rundt i
stigende flygtige og flexible mønstre,

slot som

mennesker, dyr, guder,
arbejde, ensomhed,
babel og elfen

drager igennem.

Mit ansigt udadtil, dét vasker jeg i det, der strømmer forbi.

URSULA ANDKJÆR OLSEN

translated by Katrine Øgaard Jensen
from *Third-Millennium Heart*

The third-millennium heart is a
place of many chambers

complex being with bridges and passages
transporting bodies around
increasingly fleeting and flexible patterns

castle that

humans, animals, gods
work, loneliness
babel and ivory

move through.

My outwardly face: I wash it in whatever
streams by.

KATRINE ØGAARD JENSEN

I AM THE THIRD-MILLENNIUM HERO OF COMPROMISED INFRASTRUCTURE

Rules:

1. Run each line through various online poetry generators.
2. Swap each line of the poem with a machine-generated line.
3. Edit to keep the original form as much as possible.

I am the third-millennium hero of compromised
infrastructure, overseeing every animal
transporting bodies past my fleeing
bridges and amenable passages. I am

third-millennium hard, broadcasting my passions with
complete loneliness and flexible me-technology. I am a
third-millennium helicopter, a cock-song from hell

bringing

humans, anxieties, golf
budgets and patents

to third-millennium heel.

Let there be complex being: I summon thee with my
compliance-bell for a cup of nonconsensual
babel and iworry about you.

I AM ABSURD, AQUARIUM, ZERO-COMPROMISED

Rules:

1. Rhyme all words with the words in the previous poem
2. Keep the rhythm as much as possible
2. Keep the small words as much as possible

I am absurd, aquarium, zero-compromised.
Feeling fractured over being, in theory, a cannibal
aborting goodies, I was last seen
over ridges and unnamable passages. I am

dirt! My plutonium heart is everlasting, my fashion knows
no holiness or annexable ecology. I'll
hurt Elysium, I'll pop her a fuck-song from my well

singing

Schumann's improprieties, elf
gadgets and fragments

to birds and uranium eel.

Get her duplex fleeing: Come on, be with me in
brain-science hell, have a tub of pan-sensual
fables. I will break through

I WILL BREAK THROUGH HELL WITH BIRDS AND URANIUM ELF

Rules:

1. Combine the three previous poems into one long poem
2. Turn the long poem upside down so the last line becomes the first and the first line becomes the last
3. Create an erasure poem from the long, upside-down poem.

I will break through hell with
birds and uranium elf

singing a fuck-song from my
plutonium heart. My cannibal
aquarium for a cup of complex
budgets and golf! I am

broadcasting bridges and
bodies, fleeing
every

animal. I am the third-millennium
face: Wash it in babel and
ivory gods.

I WILL PENETRATE THE UNDERWORLD WITH MY PEACOCKS AND MY HEAVY METAL ELVES

Rule:

1. Write the same poem in other words.

I will penetrate the underworld with my
peacocks and my heavy metal elves

humming a love song from my
nuclear heart. My man-eater
fishbowl for a glass of deep
economic planning and playing on the lawns! I am

launching new paths and
torsos in all directions, to avoid
any

physical contact. I am the face

of the 21st Century: Rinse it in chaos and
gods of elephant teeth.

I WILL ERECT THE NEW PARADISE

URSULA ANDKJÆR OLSEN & KATRINE OGAARD JENSEN

jeg vil opføre det nye paradis
jeg vil bygge og indrette det
SOM en have i et udgående/indkommende fartøj
med ornamenterede vægge
med et bassin i gulvet

det er udført i lette og behagelige materialer
på væggene træder livsformer frem i relief
jeg kan mærke dem ALLE når jeg stryger hænderne hen over væggen
i bassinets gulv træder livsformer frem i relief
vandets livsformer
jeg kan mærke dem ALLE når jeg går henover bunden på mine bare
fødder

jeg kan mærke ALT

URSULA ANDKJÆR OLSEN

translated by Katrine Øgaard Jensen

from *Outgoing Vessel*

i will erect the new paradise
i will build and decorate it
LIKE a garden in an outgoing/incoming vessel
with ornamented walls
with a basin in the floor

it is made from light and pleasant materials
on the walls, lifeforms stand out in relief
i can feel them ALL when i stroke the wall with my hands
on the basin floor, lifeforms stand out in relief
the lifeforms of water
i can feel them ALL when i cross the bottom with my bare
feet

i can feel EVERYTHING

I WILL ERECT AN UNINCORPORATED TOWN
IN CLARK COUNTY, NEVADA

Rules:

1. Replace paradise with Paradise, Nevada, adjacent to the city of Las Vegas.
2. Redecorate paradise by replacing nouns or could-be nouns in the poem, using nouns that are no further than the 14th noun following the original word in the dictionary.

i will erect an unincorporated town in clark county, nevada
i will build and decorate it
LIKE a gardener in an outgoing/incoming vestibule
with ornamented wallets
with a bass in the flotation

it is made from lightning and pleasant mathematics
on the walrus, lifeforms stand out in religion
i can feel them ALL when i stroke the walrus with my handcuffs
on the bastard florist, lifeforms stand out in reluctance
the lifeforms of wattage
i can feel them ALL when i croupier the bounty with my bare
footmen

i can feel EVERYTHING

I WILL BUILD AN UNDIVIDED CITY

Rules:

1. Run the poem a couple of times through Google Translate, through very different languages, finish in Danish.
2. Build a new poem in the first poem's form from the material generated via Google Translate.
3. Translate the new Danish poem into English.

i will build an undivided city
i will make it kneel
CHOOSE a florist next time!
it is a jewel of the desert
with busses floating

it consists of clear and convincing statistics
in the belly of the walrus, life is based on religion
i can feel everything, when i hit it with my bombs
in the doubtful electric water, life is based on religion
i can feel everything, when i admire my toy
soldiers

I hear IT ALL

ALL CAN ADMIRE MY DOUBTFUL ELECTRIC RELIGION

Rules:

1. Reverse the lines of the poem.
2. Insert the previous version of the poem at the bottom of the
   reversed version.
3. Create an erasure poem from the text.

I hear IT **ALL**

soldiers
i **can** feel everything, when i **admire my** toy
in the **doubtful electric** water, life is based on **religion**
i can **feel** everything, when i hit **it** with my bombs
in the belly of the walrus, **life** is based on religion
it consists of clear and convincing statistics

with busses floating
it **is a** jewel of the **desert**
CHOOSE a **florist** next time!
i will **make it kneel**
i will **build** an undivided city
i will make it kneel
CHOOSE **a** florist next time!
it is a **jewel** of the desert
with busses floating

it consists of clear and convincing statistics
in the belly of the **walrus**, life is based on religion
i can **feel** everything, when i hit it with my bombs
in the doubtful electric water, life is based on religion
i can feel **everything**, when i admire my toy
soldiers

I hear IT ALL

HEAR IT SOLDIERS

Rules:

1. Remove the erasure poem and let the rest be.
2. Create a new erasure poem from the text.

hear IT soldiers
i feel everything, when i toy in the water

life is based on
clear
jewelS

next time
i will
i will
i will make it
clear and convincing

in the belly of the electric toy
I hear IT ALL

WHILE I DREAM OF ESCAPING EVERYTHING HORRIFIC IN THE HEAD

BABA BADJI & KATRINE OGAARD JENSEN

LUKSUS ER KULTUR OG NATUR

Kulturen, naturen, disse to, de gnubbede imod hinanden, indtil livets bue dannedes.

Kulturen løser naturen fra det naturlige mådehold og lader babel = tårnene vokse, lader spirene blive rødere og rødere, ødselt, imens jeg drømmer om at slippe for

*kompliceret væsen med broer og passager til at
transportere legemer rundt i
stigende flygtige og flexible mønstre*

længes efter, at lade livet vise sig for mig i al sin enkelhed, uden luksus og infrastruktur, uden dødsforagt og institutioner, skyller naturen op igennem

*slottene,
tårnene,
dig,
mig*

med umådeholden kraft. Kulturen er overflødig = luksus.

Kulturen er livsnødvendige stopklodser for naturen = elfenben, den dræner underlaget, så

*jeg,
du,
tårnene,
slottene*

har en grund at stå på, kulturen er nødvendig = naturen er en luksus, mennesket ikke kan tillade sig.

Kulturen, naturen, disse to, de bliver ved med at gnubbe.

URSULA ANDKJÆR OLSEN

translated by Katrine Øgaard Jensen

from *Third-Millennium Heart*

LUXURY IS CULTURE AND NATURE

Culture, nature: the two rubbed against each other
until the arc of life was created.

Culture releases nature from its natural moderation, letting babel =
towers grow, letting spires become redder and redder, lavishly
while I dream of escaping this

complex being with bridges and passages
transporting bodies around
increasingly fleeting and flexible patterns

I long for life to reveal itself to me, in all its simplicity
without luxury and infrastructure, without machismo and institutions
nature washes through

castles
towers
you
me

with excessive force. Culture is superfluous = luxury.

Culture is a vital obstacle for nature = ivory. It drains
the foundation so

I
you
towers
castles

have a base to stand on. Culture is necessary = nature is a luxury
humans cannot afford.

Culture, nature: the two continue rubbing.

Rules:

1. When in mistranslation, the act of being unfaithful inspires creativity.
2. When in mistranslation, the act of daring the syntax and the expression creates a new voice and being.
3. When in mistranslation, we curate multilingualism.
4. When in mistranslation, we are unfolding language to create and reveal new meaning.

CULTURE AND NATURE ARE LUXURIOUS FAITHS

Culture et nature—they rubbed against each other
until their arc of life—*une vie est* née

culture frees nature from moderation,
letting babel's towers grow older, mythic, and mighty
letting spires become *de plus en plus rouge,*

while I dream of escaping everything horrific in the head,

être *complexe avec des viaducs et des passages*
transportant des corps
des portraits de plus en plus éphémères *et* élastiques

In all its simplicity, deep longing unveils life's mysteries
J'aspire à ce que la vie se dévoile à moi
without luxury and infrastructure
without machismo and institutions
nature washes through the fast-cooling earth

castles
châteaux
tours
toi
me
moi

in good faith and with excessive force,
culture is superfluous, luxurious, and queer
culture really gets in the way of nature
in these lush ivory towers draining to crush its stability
our rich queerness

moi
toi
towers
châteaux

want a base to stand on, culture is necessary
nature is not gratuitous, luxurious, and queer
humans cannot afford to annihilate them forever

culture & nature are enduring and rubbing

Rules:

1. When in mistranslation, we recycle material to build a new form.
2. When in mistranslation, we let lines evolve organically.
3. When in mistranslation, we become hyperlingual in collaboration.
4. When in mistranslation, non-English words can infiltrate without italicized warning.

LUXURY IS NON-ARTIFICIAL CULTURE AND NATURE

Kulturen, naturen—one robbed the other
until the arc of life was created (dictated) by

generated passages transporting bodies
des portraits de plus en plus éphémères et élastiques

Non-artificial culture and nature = the true luxury
humans cannot afford.

I long for life to re-real itself to me,
in good faith and with excessive force—

superfluous, luksuriøst and queer. Without machismo
and institutions, we might have a base to stand on

letting babel, the towers become de plus en plus rouge,
castles, tårne, du, moi.

Kunstig kultur, kunstig natur:
the two continue robbing.

Rules:

1. When in mistranslation, we scavenge the remains of language for new meaning.
2. When in mistranslation, we invite the imagined eyes to ponder.
3. When in mistranslation, we ask the imagined ear to collaborate with distance.
4. When in mistranslation, we open space for dialectal infiltration and fractured italics.

ARTIFICIAL CULTURE AND NATURE ARE NOT LUXURY

The trick for (Kulturen)
bids for translating nature
that won't plead for incursion,
other poetic authenticity
until the arc of life is crafted
uttered by a celestial syntax

generated boulevards
carrying bodies at dusk
des visages de plus en plus
brefs et souples

non-artificial *Seytaneeji njidaa*
culture and nature *maa ngi comprendree*
the true luxury *Seytaneeji njidda*
humans cannot afford to kill me
maa gni liggéey ak khêwal

lengthen my femur, tibia & fibula
for life to re-live itself in my body,
Maa gni mâgg, dinna mâgg, yeena gni mâgg,
in virtuous reliance and gratuitous strength—

superfluous, luksuriøst and queer. Without machismo
there are no breaks, there are no tears, there is love,
and bodies, in bodies, we might have a base to stand on

towers of Babel dying de plus en plus rouge
castles, tårne, du—moi—long graffiti for a beggar's memo.

Kunstig kultur, kunstig natur:
espace, légitime, colonisation bilingue
the two continue robbing *liberté.*

Rules:

1. When in mistranslation, we delete colonial languages.

[

[
[
[
[
[
[

[
[
[
[

[*Seytaneeji njidaa*
[*maa ngi comprendree*
[*Seytaneeji njidda*
[
maa gni liggéey ak khêwal

[
[
Maa gni mâgg, dinna mâgg, yeena gni mâgg
[

[
[
[

[
[

[
[
[

GAMES FOR POET-TRANSLATORS

URSULA ANDKJÆR OLSEN & KATRINE OGAARD JENSEN

ARACHNOSCIENTIFIC SALVATION
A GAME OF MISTRANSLATION SOLITAIRE

1. Start a game of online Spider Solitaire.
2. Now assign a book of poetry to three of the four suits. The last suit should be assigned to your own imagination (Dealer's Choice). I picked my English translations of Ursula Andkjær Olsen's trilogy:

   Spades (♠): *Third-Millennium Heart*
   Clubs (♣): *Outgoing Vessel*
   Hearts (♥): *My Jewel Box*
   Diamonds (♦): Dealer's Choice

3. For each card facing up, take the book matching its suit and turn the number of pages on the card. Upon reaching a page, pick one or two lines that emit spider energy and weave the text into a new poem. Continue this process with each upward-facing card until all are incorporated into your new creation.

at all times
a sensation of intricate webs
soft, possibly smooth, and heavy

life does not mean the same to them as it does to us:
i lie on their sweat-embroidery

i am allowed to be upset here
fully plugged in
glistening and inaccessible

i eat everything and i am everything:
a garden of marble
between ornamented walls

URSULA ANDKJÆR OLSEN

EVERYBODY HAS A RIGHT TO FIND JOY
IN THE PRACTICALITY OF DAILY LIFE
A DIVINATION GAME-POEM

`   1. Turn each line of the poem into a question:

what happens at all times?
what gives me a sensation of intricate webs?
what is soft, possibly smooth, and heavy?

does life not mean the same to them as it does to us?
do i lie on their sweat-embroidery?

am i allowed to be upset here?
am i fully plugged in?
am i glistening and inaccessible?

do i eat everything and become everything?
where is the garden of marble
between ornamented walls?

2. Now answer the questions by asking a tarot deck of cards:

what happens at all times?

a sister in a green, green dress is carrying something new at all times

what gives me a sensation of intricate webs?

the sun, the cunt, the navel, the web of rays and fingers
and a flower wreath give me the sensation of intricate webs

what is soft, possibly smooth, and heavy?

cups filled with water, under the water surface

does life not mean the same to them as it does to us?

the window in my lower abdomen tells me that each life is equally
important

do i lie on their sweat-embroidery?

a father in the earth tells me everybody has a right to find joy in the
practicality of daily life

am i allowed to be upset here?

i am a part of the universe, the universe will hold my rage

am i fully plugged in?

i'm plugged into the circuit of love, you are filling and emptying my cup
of life

am i glistening and inaccessible?

i am accessible, connected to a rainbow! connected to wings in the air!
all colors!

do i eat everything and am i everything?

i eat truth and I become truth, wings swirl through me also when i fight

where is the garden of marble
between ornamented walls?

all things material are moving into alignment, pointing at the right work
and the right skills

3. Now build a new poem from the answers (allow some cutting and/or expansion of the lines):

a sister in a green, green dress is carrying something new at all times
the sun, the cunt, the navel, the web of rays and fingers
and a flower wreath give me the sensation of intricate webs
cups filled with water, under the water surface

the window in my lower abdomen tells me that each life is equally important
a father in the earth tells me everybody has a right to find joy in the practicality of daily life

i am part of the universe, the universe will hold my rage and my purple air
i'm plugged into the circuit of love, you are filling and emptying my cup of life

i am accessible, connected to a rainbow! connected to wings in the air! all colors!
i eat truth and i become truth, wings swirl through me also when i fight
all things material are moving into alignment, pointing at the right work and the right skills

FIRST-PERSON LOOTER
A FRANKENSTEIN TRANSLATION GAME

1. Dismember the poem and reassemble it to form a new creature:

the sun, the cunt, the navel
the web of rays and fingers
a flower-wreath sensation
will hold my rage

plugged into the circuit
connected to a rainbow
connected to wings in the air

all colors
swirl through me also when i fight
moving into alignment

2. Now create a crossword puzzle by making each line of the new poem a clue. Loot Mary Shelley's *Frankenstein* for answers and deposit these into the word bank of your puzzle.

3. The final mistranslation is the reader's creation:

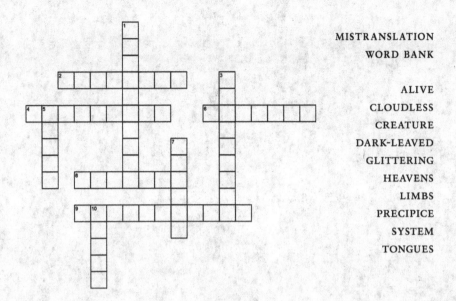

DOWN

1. all colors
3. connected to a rainbow
5. plugged into the circuit
7. the web of rays and fingers
10. the sun, the cunt, the navel

ACROSS

2. will hold my rage
4. connected to wings in the air
6. swirl through me also when i fight
8. moving into alignment
9. a flower-wreath sensation

Jeg skal være den, jeg bliver til.

URSULA ANDKJÆR OLSEN,
Det 3. artusindes hjerte

I must be who I become.

URSULA ANDKJÆR OLSEN,
Third-Millennium Heart
translated by Katrine Øgaard Jensen

To Ursula Andkjær Olsen, for generously being "med på spøgen," for our many explorations and exchanges, for the wreaths of borrowed materials.

To Sawako Nakayasu, for insisting that these experiments should become a book, for being a vital inspiration, collaborator, and guide in poetry and (mis)translation, and for selecting "Arachnoscientific Salvation" for the Academy of American Poets' *Poem-a-Day*.

To Aditi Machado, Baba Badji, Paul Cunningham, and CAConrad, for supporting and elevating this book with their expansive approaches to poetry and translation.

To Sarabande editor in chief Kristen Renee Miller, for bringing her dedicated vision as a poet-translator to the completion of this manuscript, and to the entire Sarabande team for all their effort and care.

To Action Books editors Johannes Göransson, Joyelle McSweeney, Katherine Hedeen, and Paul Cunningham (again), for publishing and continuing to support Olsen's work in corrupted and (rarely) uncorrupted translation.

To *BOMB* editor Raluca Albu, for her editorial prowess and immense support, and for publishing the sections "I Will Erect the New Paradise," "I Place the World," "It Is You Who Corrupt My Rayless Corpus," and "When the Beginning Feels Like an Ending, There Are Signs" in a special Mistranslation Series. To the *BOMB* editors for nominating "I Will Erect the New Paradise" for a Pushcart Prize.

To Anton Hur, Jeremy Tiang, and Jennifer Croft, for publishing "Retranslating Poetry with Runes: A Ritual for Poet-Translators" in their bold and brilliant Translation Folio in *The Keyon Review*'s Spring 2023 issue.

To *Berkeley Poetry Review* editor 최 Lindsay and *Ordkonst* editor Erik

Isberg, for publishing the section "Compromised Infrastructure" in their joint issue of poems, translations, and experiments in collaboration, which began the mistranslation project in 2018.

To the Danish Arts Foundation, for supporting my translations and mistranslations of *Third-Millennium Heart*, *Outgoing Vessel*, and *My Jewel Box*.

To the life-giving and ever-inspiring Susan Bernofsky, without whom I would never have made it through the (as Anton Hur accurately calls it) 'Emerging Literary Translator Valley of Death.'

To Chukwuma Ndulue, for his invaluable guidance and feedback on Olsen's trilogy in English, and to Bonnie Chau, Liza St. James, Ari Braverman, Kayla Maiuri, Lillian Klein, and Orien Longo — my collaborators in everything.

—Allahverdi, Arash. *ConQuest*. Translated by Ali Araghi. Co•im•press, 2022.

—Andkjær Olsen, Ursula. *My Jewel Box*. Translated by Katrine Øgaard Jensen. Action Books, 2022.

—Andkjær Olsen, Ursula. *Outgoing Vessel*. Translated by Katrine Øgaard Jensen. Action Books, 2021.

—Andkjær Olsen, Ursula. *Third-Millennium Heart*. Translated by Katrine Øgaard Jensen. Action Books/Broken Dimanche Press, 2017.

—Arsanios, Mirene. *Notes on Mother Tongues*. Ugly Duckling Presse, 2020.

—Badji, Baba. *Ghost Letters*. Parlor Press, 2021.

—Berg, Aase. *Hackers*. Translated by Johannes Göransson. Black Ocean, 2017.

—Bhanot, Kavita, and Jeremy Tiang, eds. *Violent Phenomena: 21 Essays on Translation*. Tilted Axis Press, 2022.

—Brown, Brandon. *Flowering Mall*. Roof Books, 2012.

—Cameron, David. *Flowers of Bad*. Ugly Duckling Presse, 2007.

—Carson, Anne. *Float*. Alfred A. Knopf, 2016.

—CAConrad. *Advanced Elvis Course*. Soft Skull Press, 2008/Peninsula Press, 2024.

—CAConrad. *AMANDA PARADISE: Resurrect Extinct Vibration*. Wave Books, 2021.

—CAConrad. *A Beautiful Marsupial Afternoon: New (Soma)tics*. Wave Books, 2012.

—CAConrad. *Deviant Propulsion*. Soft Skull Press, 2006.

—CAConrad. *ECODEVIANCE: (Soma)tics for the Future Wilderness*. Wave Books, 2014.

—CAConrad. *Listen to the Golden Boomerang Return*. Wave Books/ UK Penguin, 2024.

—CAConrad. *The Book of Frank*. Wave Books, 2010/UK Penguin, 2023.

—CAConrad. *While Standing in Line for Death*. Wave Books, 2017.

—CAConrad. *You Don't Have What It Takes to Be My Nemesis and Other (Soma)tics*. UK Penguin, 2023.

—Charles, Jos. *feeld*. Milkweed Editions, 2018.

—Cohen, Sharmila, and Paul Legault, eds. *The Sonnets: Translating and Rewriting Shakespeare*. Nightboat Books, 2013.

—Croft, Jennifer. "Why Translators Should Be Named on Book Covers." *The Guardian*. September 10, 2021. https://www.theguardian.com/books/2021/sep/10/why-translators-should-be-named-on-book-covers

—Croft, Jennifer, Jeremy Tiang, and Anton Hur, eds. "Translation Folio." Special issue, *Kenyon Review* 45, no. 2 (Spring 2023).

—Cunningham, Paul. *Fall Garment*. Schism Press, 2022.

—Cunningham, Paul. *The House of the Tree of Sores*. Schism Press, 2020.

—Cunningham, Paul. *The Inmost*. Carrion Bloom Books, 2020.

—Cunningham, Paul. *Sociocide at the 24/7*. New Michigan Press, 2025.

—Choi, Don Mee. "Darkness—Translation—Migration." *Featured Blogger* (blog). *Poetry Foundation*, April 6, 2016. https://www.poetryfoundation.org/featured-blogger/74798/darkness-translation-migration

—Choi, Don Mee. *DMZ Colony*. Wave Books, 2020.

—Choi, Don Mee. *Hardly War*. Wave Books, 2016.

—Choi, Don Mee. *Mirror Nation*. Wave Books, 2024.

—Choi, Don Mee. *Translation is a Mode=Translation is an Anti-neocolonial Mode*. Ugly Duckling Presse, 2020.

—Göransson, Johannes. *Summer*. Tarpaulin Sky Press, 2022.

—Göransson, Johannes. *Transgressive Circulation: Essays on Translation*. Noemi Press, 2018.

—Göransson, Johannes, and Sara Tuss Efrik. *The New Quarantine*. Inside the Castle, 2023.

—Hawkey, Christian. *Ventrakl*. Ugly Duckling Presse, 2010.

—Hemphill, Destiny. *motherworld: a devotional for the alter-life*. Action Books, 2023.

—H. Kaza, Madhu, ed. "Kitchen Table Translation." Special issue, *Aster(ix) Journal*, Summer 2017.

—H. Kaza, Madhu. *Lines of Flight*. Ugly Duckling Presse, 2024.

—LaNay, Sade. *Härte*. Downstate Legacies, 2018.

—Legault, Paul. *The Tower*. Coach House Books, 2020.

—Long Soldier, Layli. *Whereas*. Graywolf Press, 2017.

—Machado, Aditi. *Emporium*. Nightboat Books, 2020.

—Machado, Aditi. *The End*. Ugly Duckling Presse, 2020.

—Machado, Aditi. *Material Witness*. Nightboat Books, 2024.

—Machado, Aditi. *Some Beheadings*. Nightboat Books, 2017.

—McSweeney, Joyelle. *The Necropastoral: Poetry, Media, Occults*. University of Michigan Press, 2014.

—McSweeney, Joyelle, and Johannes Göransson. *Deformation Zone*. Ugly Duckling Presse, 2012.

—M. Hedeen, Katherine. "Dismantling the Myth of Originality: Translation, Collaboration, Solidarity." *Action Books Blog*, April 28, 2020. https://actionbooks.org/2020/04/dismantling-the-myth-of-originality-translation-collaboration-solidarity-by-katherine-m-hedeen/

—M. Hedeen, Katherine. "Manifesto?" *Asymptote*, April 2019. https://www.asymptotejournal.com/special-feature/katherine-hedeen-manifesto/

—M. Hedeen, Katherine, and Zoë Skoulding, eds. *Poetry's Geographies: A Transatlantic Anthology of Translations*. Eulalia Books, 2023.

—Nakayasu, Sawako. "The Errant Translator: Field Notes." *Words Without Borders*, January 9, 2024. https://wordswithoutborders.org/read/article/2024-01/the-errant-translator-field-notes-sawako-nakayasu/

—Nakayasu, Sawako. *Mouth: Eats Color: Sagawa Chika Translations, Anti-Translations and Originals*. Rogue Factorial, 2011.

—Nakayasu, Sawako. *Pink Waves*. Omnidawn, 2023.

—Nakayasu, Sawako. *Say Translation Is Art*. Ugly Duckling Presse, 2020.

—Nakayasu, Sawako. *Some Girls Walk into the Country They Are From*. Wave Books, 2020.

—Nao, Vi Khi. *God Expects You to Collaborate with Infinity*. Business Bear Press, 2017.

—Nao, Vi Khi. *Sheep Machine*. Black Sun Lit, 2018.

—Nguyen, Diana Khoi. *Ghost Of*. Omnidawn, 2018.

—Park Hong, Cathy. *Dance Dance Revolution*. W. W. Norton, 2007.

—Philip, M. NourbeSe. *Zong!* Wesleyan University Press, 2008

—Pizarnik, Alejandra. *Extracting the Stone of Madness: Poems 1962–1972*. Translated by Yvette Siegert. New Directions, 2016.

—Pizarnik, Alejandra. *A Tradition of Rupture: Selected Critical Writings*. Translated by Cole Heinowitz. Ugly Duckling Presse, 2019.

—Renee Miller, Kristen. "dachte er, es war kein." *Poetry*, May 2022. https://www.poetryfoundation.org/poetrymagazine/poems/157711/dachte-er-es-war-kein

—Renee Miller, Kristen. "nous nous baignons—variations." *The Nation*, December 28, 2023. https://www.thenation.com/article/culture/nous-nous-baignons-variations/

—Rilke, Rainer Maria. *Duino Elegies*. Translated by Edward Snow. North Point Press, 2001.

—Robert-Foley, Lily. *Experimental Translation: The Work of Translation in the Age of Algorithmic Production*. Goldsmiths Press, 2024.

—Sappho. *If Not, Winter: Fragments of Sappho*. Translated by Anne Carson. Vintage Books, 2002.

—Serres, Michel. *The Five Senses: A Philosophy of Mingled Bodies*. Translated by Margaret Sankey and Peter Cowley. Continuum, 2009.

—Wolf, Uljana. *Subsisters: Selected Poems*. Translated by Sophie Seita. Belladonna* Collaborative, 2017.

—최 Lindsay. *Transverse*. Futurepoem, 2021.

—최 Lindsay, and Erik Isberg, eds. "An Issue of Poems, Translations, and Experiments in Collaboration." Special issue, *Ordkonst x Berkeley Poetry Review*, 2018. https://ordkonstxbpr.weebly.com

KATRINE ØGAARD JENSEN is a poet and translator of Danish litera-ture. She is the recipient of several fellowships and awards, including the National Translation Award in Poetry, the Kenyon Review's Peter Taylor Fellowship, the Danish Arts Foundation's Young Artistic Elite Fellow-ship, and Kjeld Elfelt's Memorial Grant from the Danish Translators' Association, and has been a finalist for the Best Translated Book Award and the PEN Award for Poetry in Translation. Her translations include *Third-Millennium Heart* (Action Books, 2017), *Outgoing Vessel* (Action Books, 2021), and *My Jewel Box* (Action Books, 2022), all by Ursula Andkjær Olsen, as well as *To The Most Beautiful* by Mette Moestrup (co•im•press, 2024). Previously, she taught Creative Writing and Liter-ary Translation at Columbia University, where she also served as Acting Director of Literary Translation at Columbia (LTAC) from 2019 through 2020. Jensen currently serves as Executive Director of the American Literary Translators Association (ALTA).

URSULA ANDKJÆR OLSEN (b. Copenhagen, 1970) is a poet and author. She holds a master's degree in musicology and philosophy from Technische Universität Berlin and the University of Copenhagen. She made her literary debut in 2000 with the poetry collection *Lulu's Songs* and *Speeches* (Lindhardt og Ringhof) and has since published eleven poetry collections. Her three most recent collections—*Third-Millennium Heart, Outgoing Vessel,* and *My Jewel Box*—have been translated into English by Katrine Øgaard Jensen and published by Action Books. From 2016 to 2023, Andkjær Olsen was affiliated with the Danish Academy of Creative Writing, first as a permanent teacher and later as principal. She has received numerous awards and distinctions, most recently the Prince Henrik Prize in 2024. In April 2017, she was awarded a lifelong honorary grant from the Danish Arts Foundation. She is a member of the Danish Academy. For more information, visit www.ursulaandkjaerolsen.dk.

SAWAKO NAKAYASU is an artist working with language, performance, and translation—separately and combined. Recent books include *Pink Waves* (Omnidawn, 2023), *Some Girls Walk Into The Country They Are From* (Wave Books, 2020) and the pamphlet *Say Translation Is Art* (Ugly Duckling Presse, 2020). Translations include *The Collected Poems of Chika Sagawa* (Modern Library, 2020), as well as *Mouth: Eats Color—Sagawa Chika Translations, Anti-Translations, & Originals* (Rogue Factorial, 2011), a multilingual work of both original and translated poetry. *Settle Her,* which was written on the #1 bus line in Providence on Thanksgiving Day of 2017 on the occasion of her cutting ties with normative Thanksgiving celebrations, is forthcoming from Solid Objects. She teaches poetry, translation, and interdisciplinary art in the Literary Arts department at Brown University.

PAUL CUNNINGHAM co-manages Action Books. He is the author of *Sociocide at the 24/7* (New Michigan Press, 2025), *Fall Garment* (Schism Press, 2022), and *The House of the Tree of Sores* (Schism Press, 2020). New writing has most recently appeared in *Ballast Journal, Annulet, BOMB, Mercury Firs, Amsterdam Review,* and others. His translation of Sara Tuss Efrik's play *Danse Macabre Piggies* was anthologized in *Experimental Writing: A Writer's Guide and Anthology* (Bloomsbury, 2024). Cunningham's poem-films have screened in museums and festivals in Mexico, India, Denmark, and Czechia. He currently manages the MFA in Creative Writing program at the University of Notre Dame.

CACONRAD has worked with the ancient technologies of poetry and ritual since 1975. Their latest book is *Listen to the Golden Boomerang*

Return (Wave Books / UK Penguin 2024). They received the Ruth Lilly Poetry Prize, a PEN Josephine Miles Award, a Creative Capital grant, a Pew Fellowship, and a Lambda Award. *The Book of Frank* is now available in 9 different languages, and they coedited *SUPPLICATION: Selected Poems of John Wieners* (Wave Books). They exhibit poems as art objects with recent solo shows in Tucson, Arizona, as well as in Spain and Portugal. They teach at the Sandberg Art Institute in Amsterdam. Please visit them at https://linktr.ee/CAConrad88

ADITI MACHADO is the author of three books of poetry—*Material Witness* (2024), *Emporium* (2020), and *Some Beheadings* (2017)—from Nightboat Books and translator of Farid Tali's novel *Prosopopoeia* (Action Books, 2016). Her writing appears in journals like *Annulet*, *BOMB*, *Chicago Review*, *jubilat*, *Lana Turner*, *Volt*, and *Western Humanities Review*, as well as in chapbook form. A recipient of the James Laughlin and Believer Poetry Awards, Machado teaches at the University of Cincinnati.

BABA BADJI is a Senegalese American poet, translator, and researcher whose work explores a rich array of postcolonial studies. His interdisciplinary approach merges various theoretical frameworks and engages deeply with the vibrant debates surrounding postcolonial critical translation theory and Négritude poetics, contributing to a nuanced understanding of these concepts within both Anglophone and Francophone worlds. He is fluent in English, French, Wolof, Manding, and Diola and weaves them into his poetry and translations, enhancing the textures and dimensions of his creative and critical thinking. His first full-length poetry manuscript, *Ghost Letters*, was longlisted for the 2021 National Book Awards (Parlor Press, 2021). Through his work, Badji continues illuminating the intricate connections between language, culture, and identity.

SARABANDE BOOKS is a nonprofit independent literary press head-quartered in Louisville, Kentucky. Established in 1994 to champion poetry, fiction, and essay, we are committed to creating lasting editions that honor exceptional writing. With over two hundred titles in print, we have earned a dedicated readership and a national reputation as a publisher of diverse forms and innovative voices.

www.ingramcontent.com/pod-product-compliance
Lightning Source LLC
Chambersburg PA
CBHW010347110925
32361CB00016B/139